Withering forests
Dying rivers

Withering forests
Dying rivers

A call for collective action to preserve, protect and rejuvenate our forest cover, water bodies and natural resources.

Naba Bhattacharjee

PARTRIDGE

To order additional copies of this book, contact
Partridge India
000 800 919 0634 (Call Free)
+91 000 80091 90634 (Outside India)
orders.india@partridgepublishing.com

www.partridgepublishing.com/india

This book is dedicated to my mother (L) Kiron Bala, wife Yolanda and daughters Namrata, Navneeta & Nayanika – all of whom has been source of inspiration and motivation, each in their innate individual manner.

Gratitude to (L) Silverine Swer, Patricia Mukhim, Sunita Narain, and host of friends, relatives and well wishers who had trust in my humble efforts in mobilizing public opinion to protect our environment and conserve our forest.

Contents

Preface ix

1 Umiam Lake faces extinction blues............ 1
2 Ailing environment & sick planners........... 9
3 Our defiled environment........................14
4 Where has all the rain gone?.................... 20
5 Let "Save Rivers" initiative begin
     from our home.................................. 25
6 Water conservation Or Dry and
     barren future...31
7 Nature's fury, man's agony. 42
8 Mining on sustained yield principle. 48
9 Sharing spoils of mining. 54
10 Spare the pine trees; use the pine needles. ... 59
11 Methodical & eco-friendly urban
      planning.. 64
12 Monsoon mayhem and waste
      management. 72
13 Violation of law; elusive penalty............... 81
14 Redefining forest to ensure
      unimpeded deforestation?..................... 86
15 Dangers of exploiting ground water. 92
16 Conserve water in nature's bucket!........... 98

17 Harvest rain water to check wet
    desert syndrome. 107

18 Resurgence of traditional medicines. 113

19 Unsung nature conservationists.............. 122

20 Harnessing renewable energy. 133

21 NGT ban on coal mining -
    a substantive issue of environment,
    safety and health. 140

22 World environment day celebration –
    mere symbolism?................................150

23 Echoes of climate variation. 153

24 Endangered catchments & water bodies!....158

25 Mitigation and climate change................166

26 Tribulations of mechanical mining. 172

27 Green finance & sustainability. 176

28 Forest policy and management................184

29 Traditional wisdom & young
    environment brigade. 190

30 Clean environment; better pandemic
    resilience! 194

31 Bridging the inequality of "balance".......199

About the Author 207

Preface

It was a late afternoon in the summer of 2004. I was finally returning to my home; my birthplace – Shillong, capital of Meghalaya, a state in India. The homecoming, midway of a promising career of almost two decades, was a conscious decision, in response to an inner call. The prompting of the inner call grew louder every time I came home on short holidays. I was missing something unexplained. It was like a plant extricated, just when it was striking roots. I was not willing to add foliage and canopy anymore in alien soil but start from where I left behind, threads of my childhood memories amongst familiar faces and places.

That afternoon, as I stood under an *Acacia* tree on the road near the picturesque Umiam Lake, nestled among green hills at an altitude of over 4000 feet, the burden of that inner voice was off my chest. I took a deep breath and could clearly discern the known aroma – a blend of the soil, vegetation and gently blowing breeze. I was home finally. I did not want to lose time in my rewind journey and begin from where the link snapped. I decided to go to the infamous "old road" en route, which use to be the end point to one of our favourite school trekking trail. We learnt from elders then that the old road was the original British alignment of Shillong Guwahati road, prior to independence of India; which was submerged during construction of the Umiam Lake in 1958, post independence, to be replaced by the present alternate alignment.

As I stood barefoot in the waters, where the old road plunges into the lake, reminiscing of the bygone days, reality struck me in the face together with a cold draught sprinkled with a light drizzle. To my horror a pile of garbage, plastic bottles and host of other materials came floating. I retracted from the water and immediately felt grime and oily substance on both my feet which was grey from the greasy slick.

It was not the same crystal clear water where the shades of green from the adjoining foliage on banks or even one's own shadow could be easily discernible in the waters of the lake, on any sunny day. It was then. Not anymore today.

Water has been polluted and poisoned. The lush green forest cover of both sub-tropical and moist deciduous type are receding while the lower storey vegetation were reduced to sparse patches, exposing the red soil of the gentle undulating hills and dales. I wanted to go to the bottom of how all this had happened. It was as if a hurricane of great intensity had struck with ferocity.

In the course of my study the grim reality unravelled in matter of few months. The entire eco system was ailing. I realized that we were at the cross roads for going against the social tenets laid down by our forefathers. Their vision or rather practical wisdom lies shattered among the ruins of unregulated mining, clogged rivers, and deforested land rendered barren, hill sides ravaged and razed to the ground, polluted water bodies et al. This generation has utterly failed the preceding and succeeding generations. All of us are to blame for this devastation which stares us in the face today. And primarily because we were mute spectators to the all round destruction which goes on unabated. We failed to protest against those who sold out our pristine environment through mining of fossil fuels, abetting and conniving in destruction of our untouched forest and rich bio diversity. Natural wealth and resources has been bartered away compromising the basic needs and interest of the common man. Our river systems and water bodies are more of cess pools, and dumping ground. History is replete with examples of how rivers are intricately linked to a civilization; the tradition and custom of a community of people. And look what we have converted our symbols of pride into. We have witnessed innumerable agitations and protests on every issue under the sun except for conserving our heritage of nature's bounty, bestowed on the state generously and assiduously guarded by traditional wisdom. This generation has no answers for the coming generations, whom we have pushed to the brink of disaster.

I decided to highlight the issues in my own humble manner by drawing attention of those who matter ranging from politicians, government officials, civil society members, students and others. I tried to reach out through writings, columns discussions, presentations, public interest litigations et al. It was not only flagging problems but also trying to provide possible solutions or educing suggestions and debate in the society.

After fifteen long years it is ironic but true that no appreciable change or rather improvement in any of the spheres has taken place. All the alerts and warnings remain mostly unheeded.

This work of non-fiction is another effort; another attempt to focus attention on the issue of healing our sick environment. I am sure many of the issues will find resonance in the varying level of environment desecration taking place all over the world.

It is only but natural that I begin with Umiam Lake which opened my eyes to the grim reality and unfolding of the environment desecration saga in my state.

The contents reflect some of the key environment denigrating issues highlighted since start of the millennium.

Many of the acts and rules together with other statistics reflected in the articles may have changed over the last two decades but the core issues still persist.

Unfortunately most alerts remain unheeded and unattended even to-day!.

1

Umiam Lake faces extinction blues.

(Issue highlighted in the year 2004)

The Umiam Lake near Shillong, located in Meghalaya state of India is one of the most picturesque and popular tourist spot of the region. It could well have been developed into a premier destination in the country, with proper vision and planning. A turnaround is still possible, since the subject of tourism is gradually emerging from the confines of seminar and arm chair rhetoric, to be actually recognized as a prospective sector for economic resurgence of the region. The Umiam Lake, spread over an area of around 10 sq km, also has a unique distinction of being primarily an artificial reservoir of the first Hydel Project of the North East. This ambitious venture which commenced in the year 1960 was commissioned five years later. It was a rare phenomenon, particularly in the 1960's for an individual project to possess supplementary economic potential of such magnitude, in addition to its primary objective. This project, until recently was meeting a substantial power requirement of most north eastern states.

It is thus ironic that Umiam Lake – an engineering marvel, is facing the danger of extinction. The threat has not emanated due to any technological flaw in construction, but from a host of external factors impinging directly on the life of the reservoir. The principal factors responsible are the colossal flow of sediment, silt, sewage and multiple pollutants into the lake, from the catchments. The life of the dam was estimated to be around 200 years at the time of commissioning. Yet hydrographic survey, water quality analysis, catchment assessment including sediment flow rate data, reveal the astounding fact that Umiam lake will not survive for more than 30 to 35 years, if existing situation continues unabated.

The principal catchment area of the Lake and Dam is spread over 220 sq km which includes Shillong and adjoining areas, besides portion of Ri Bhoi District. The topography of the catchments is hilly with long drawn deep gorges and ravines. The entire region has undergone extensive environmental degradation and loss of forest cover. A vast tract of the catchments area is open with grasses, broom sticks and occasional patches of ground cover comprising of "lower storey" vegetation, while the other parts are covered with open and degraded forests. The locale is heavily leeched with conspicuous formation of gullies in the open areas, devoid of vegetative cover. This is a continuous process, destabilizing the soil profile and structure. The shrinking of this invaluable natural resource has adversely affected the ecological stability and environmental security. The impact of human activities and the increasing pace of development, have led to serious ecological repercussions which have been caused mainly by - a). Increase in population leading to diverse patterns of land utilization by destruction of forests. b). Deforestation for commercial, pastoral and agronomic activities c). Cultivation, including shifting, in sub-marginal lands without regard to land capability, soil and water conservation). Modern unplanned development especially of roads and communications as also unscientific mining and quarrying.

A combination of these factors has been causing severe erosion, extensive runoff, land degradation, widespread silting up of drainage channels reducing their capacity to canalize rainfall runoff. This has resulted in haphazard movement of water from the catchments located in the higher ridges to the Lake situated in the valley, carrying with it large volume of eroded materials to the dam. There are multiple networks of seasonal and perennial streams and rivulets spread all throughout the catchments. During summer these streams and rivulets are over flooded and they discharge either into Umkhrah or Umshyrpi, originating from the higher ridges of Shillong plateau. These seasonal canals together, in co-ordination with the streams and rivulets transport a bulk of the soil, sewage and garbage including a host of other pollutants down to the lake.

In winter, the grasses on the hill slope become dry and occurrence of forest fire becomes a regular phenomenon, resulting in annihilation of the undergrowth. The practice of shifting cultivation, particularly growing of potato in the catchments, lead to loosening of soil structure which is ultimately washed down into the lake. The consequence is clearly evident from the reddish and murky waters of the lake in monsoon. This process has been an annual feature since decades and gaining momentum with passage of time. The dry winter months provides an insight into the extent of silt deposition in the Dam when the entire lake becomes dotted with "red islands". The numbers of such islands are increasing every winter.

In order to save the Dam and Umiam Stage-I Hydro Electric Project, it is imperative to implement tangible remedial and preventive measures simultaneously, on a sustained basis. The approach will have to be multi pronged, encompassing both short and long term strategy including administrative measures and enactment of relevant acts, irrespective of status or ownership of land, for ecological revival of the catchments. It is a universal phenomenon that, there is no substitute for well established ground vegetation and all other measures are incidental, becoming essential with depletion of this vital cover. The role of forests in controlling soil erosion requires no amplification. The essence of the rehabilitation process will have to be based on the National River Conservation Plan the guidelines of which has been prescribed by the National River Conservation Directorate, in the Ministry of Environment, Forest and Climate Change, Govt. of India and the revised guidelines issued under the National Lake Conservation Plan.

Further, the entire sewage including garbage and other pollutants from Shillong and its adjoining semi urban township and villages, located within the catchments release into respective streams and rivulets. These in turn converge at different confluence points like Mawpdung bridge or Demsiniong and empty in most cases, into either of the two rivers- Umkhrah or Umshyrpi. Meghalaya at present has no infrastructure of any manner, type or capacity for Sewage or Effluent Treatment. In addition, there are other Non Point Sources of Pollution like dairy plant, motor garages, cattle wallowing, open area and bank side defecation, dead body and carcass dumping, indiscriminate dumping of garbage, industrial solid waste, bio medical and other hazardous and toxic waste.

The gravity of the current situation demand immediate action for adopting a viable technology for treatment of sewage, effluent and other pollutants of the catchments, before draining into the Umiam Lake. A comprehensive state of the art system with products and services, which cover the entire spectrum of water and waste water treatment, has to be introduced. The principal feature of some latest technology lie in their in built capacity to remove sediment, coarse size particles, plastic, paper, rags etc present in waste water, initiating total settlement and simultaneously allowing subsequent sewage transfer. Moreover, the requirement of space, which is a major constraint in the hills, is much less compared to conventional sequencing batch transfer technology. Engineering structures need to be established as ancillary preventive measures. Simultaneously, remedial measures, primarily desiltation techniques like flushing, density current venting, sluicing etc will have to be undertaken. Dredging will be the most appropriate and effective mechanism to remove the enormous silt and other deposits. The only limiting factor of this operation is the huge financial involvement.

A number of Hydel Projects are being established all over the hilly states of north east India to harness the huge untapped hydro power potential of over 60,000MW. Arunachal Pradesh, which alone accounts for 50,000 MW, has about a dozen projects, particularly on the Subansiri and Siang rivers, either on going, ready to commence or under investigation. All such projects including those in Sikkim and Mizoram, need to learn from the Umiam Dam experience and initiate appropriate measures, from the inception stage itself. The rough and hostile terrain of the state, with high altitude is more susceptible to the vagaries of nature and biological interference. The havoc and large scale destruction caused by flash flood of mighty Siang, in matter of hours during June 2000, purportedly due to breach in a dam located in China is a case in point. The districts of Arunachal Pradesh, downstream, bordering China was devastated by the flash floods. The extent of damage in future will be of much greater magnitude and intensity in such topography, with more than one reservoir proposed to be built to dam the water of Siang.

2

Ailing environment & sick planners.

The desecration of the environment has come into sustained focus during last few decades. The encouraging aspect is that this vital issue has probably for the first time educed strong reactions from a section of the political fraternity on the gory state of our environment. The issues range from receding catchments and rapid disappearance and defilement of water bodies, high level of air pollution, threat of annihilation faced by the green hills and dales and diversion of forest areas for non forestry activities like mining and quarrying. It is too early to predict whether such environmental concerns are one of the many passing sparks witnessed earlier, which withers away almost as fast as it emerges. The situation for the last decade or more has been similar to a patient who is aware of being afflicted by a major ailment but refusing treatment firm in the belief that the situation shall ameliorate on its own. Finally a stage comes when it becomes too late for even the best corrective measure to have any impact and the countdown begins. Our environment too is ailing and is at its breaking point for a while now with the situation deteriorating with each passing day. The countdown has begun. Yet no tangible initiation except for rhetoric and empty commitment has been witnessed. There has been no positive action to arrest the rapid decline in the state of environment which has been allowed to be defiled and exploited at will. The issues which are discussed to-day are not new. They have been in existence for decades gradually assuming the alarming proportion in absence of any concrete measures to evolve a comprehensive strategy to tackle the impending holocaust. A number of NGOs & individuals have been harping for years in vain to bring a halt to the defilement. Increase in population leading to diverse patterns of land use by destruction of vegetative cover, deforestation for commercial, pastoral and agronomic activities, ignoring land capability, soil and water conservation, unplanned development and above all mining and quarrying are at the root of the ailment. Yet no remedial measures are forthcoming. It is intriguing indeed that when problems are known and multiple solutions are available to tackle the impending environmental horror, no planned corrective measures are initiated. Reactions have been mostly to ignore the warnings or bulldoze public opinion. It is indeed baffling as to why debates and deliberations related to to decisions on issues of public interest is not encouraged and adequate flexibility adopted by the planners in accommodating genuine public concern. On the contrary, the desired approach is to make all efforts to engage the civil society in convincing deliberations with an open mind to factor in rational public opinion prior to finalizing important issues. The idea is not to oppose just for the sake of opposing but unite on issues which have the potential to have adverse impact on all sections of society, directly or otherwise. There has to be a point of convergence of ideas on matters related to safeguarding the environment and bio diversity of our habitat.

It is imperative to try and decipher the reasons for the apathy and inactivity. One plausible reason is the lack of vision and effort on part of planners and their failure to evolve a suitable action plan in any sector of development. Environment issues lie at the bottom of the least priority list & receive minimum or no attention at all. In the north east region of our country, where public alertness and vigilance is virtually absent in urban locales and percentage of illiteracy coupled with general simplicity being still high in rural areas, the written word is treated with respect. The system has been so created and protected that a common man is immune to realities even in his immediate surroundings. In a country where capability and competence is generally judged by a person's educational qualifications, there is little doubt the planner is on a very safe wicket without accountability or practical experience to deliver. The political class is at the mercy of planners since in the game of playing with figures and manifesting expertise in respective field, the rules are framed by them. They take many things and other pillars of governance for granted. Plans manipulated by intelligent arm chair planners are coming out into the open. Mahatma Gandhi talked of the importance of mixing intellect with labour. Excess of intellect and virtually no labour and practical experience has turned our planner not only impractical but at the same time supremely confident that he is always right. This brings us to the question on what makes the planner superior and always allowed to have the last word. The role needs to be reversed and the person at the execution level together with members of civil society who suffer from neglect need to be heard. The channel of communication are effectively blocked on grounds that "proper channel" is a pre-requisite, which in effect means reliable and valuable inputs are not allowed to reach the right quarters. The planner has a great gift of making simple solutions look complicated and more often than not settling for inaction as the action forward.

The recent development hopefully shall usher in the unlearning process for the planners and some of their mighty political bosses which can be very traumatic as it takes immense courage and resilience to be changed by the common man whom he regards as socially and economically inferior. It is a question of time before such number grows and till then Mark Twain's words "To do good is noble. To tell others to do good is also noble but much less trouble". So it will be good that maximum members of our society take a little more trouble to do good, for the cause of common good in Meghalaya.

3

Our defiled environment.

(Issue highlighted in the year 2008)

How sick is the environment? Is it on the brink of collapse? Has exploitation of nature by man, reached a point of no return? What are the options if any to retrieve the health of our environment? These together with thousand of similar queries are howling for attention with none to take up the cause of healing the denigration of the eco-system. The last couple of decades have witnessed a world wide consciousness and introspection on environmental issues. Yet, in our state there is hardly any concern to arrest the devastation and restore environmental security. It is a long and arduous task, where even if concerted efforts to stabilize at the current level commence in right and total earnest, it will take decades to restore some parity. It is high time for the opinion makers, political masters & civil society to sit up and comprehend the catastrophe looming large in the horizon. The issues pertaining to environment is no longer the domain of a select few. There is genuine concern and concrete steps initiated in the developing and poor countries too. The impact of environmental degradation in our state is evident for all to see and feel. Human travail and tribulation like water and power scarcity, abrupt climate change, acute water and air pollution, declining water bodies, desecrated rivers and depleting ground water; recurring natural disasters et al – all manifests with clarity, the consequence of defiling the environment. The symptoms are too obvious to overlook yet there are no sign of any initiative to even delay the inevitable.

Human induced activities in our state as in other parts of the world are responsible for the momentum. The impact of the increasing quest of a small section of our society has led to serious ecological aftermath, which has been caused mainly by quantum leap in extraction and use of fossil fuels like coal, limestone and other minerals including recent resumption of deforestation, diverse land use pattern without regard to land capability, soil and water conservation. Modern unplanned construction of roads and buildings together with unscientific mining and quarrying has also contributed to the ecological denigration.

The above activities together with emissions from different sources and large scale use of harmful chemicals & pesticides have greatly increased greenhouse gas release. Activities that generate greenhouse gases are called 'sources' and those that remove them are known as 'sinks'. A balance between 'sources' and 'sinks' like forests – called 'sinks' of carbon dioxide are disappearing fast. Our rivers are highly contaminated. The pollution load on the rivers and lake system include around 35 MLD of sewage daily and a major portion of around 73 MT of total daily garbage generation of 174 MT within Greater Shillong, not disposed or treated.

There is an innate link between water and hydro power generation. Decline in water supply adversely affects generation of hydro power to its full potential. A classic example is the Umiam Hydel project resorting to continuous power cuts during lean season. All the proposed hydel projects shall meet similar fate if conservation and management of water is not accorded top priority. The problem of water crisis in spite of high rainfall, can primarily be attributed to rapid decline in the fragile resource base, impinging directly on catchments which are natures indigenous "water reservoirs". These "store houses" have been exposed to over exploitation and consequently, major catchments, all over the state are in different stages of being finally wiped out. The Meghalaya Protection of Catchment Areas Act, 1990 & Rules 1996 was enacted to provide for the protection of catchment areas and preserve water sources. The act could never be invoked due to its inherent legal deficiencies and intricate land holding system. It is imperative for the Government to review both the moribund Act & Rule by incorporating adequate legal sanctions, authority and sweeping powers as far as preservation of catchments and practical implementation of remedial measures are concerned. It is not a question of non-availability of water but a consequence of unplanned use and misuse of natural resources coupled with total ignorance and lack of initiative to conserve water. In order to overcome water stress conditions, rampant harnessing of ground water even for commercial operation is common. In order to maintain this potential, a hydraulic equilibrium must be established between availability and utilization. The proliferation of energized wells has to be restricted, since such wells deplete ground water ranging from 1 to 3 meters a year depending on their location. In hilly terrain, the decline shall be much higher. The best way to replenish ground water is through rain water management and harvesting aimed at maintaining the water table at a pre-determined constant level to which extraction has to be limited.

Mining of coal shall continue till the reserve is exhausted. By that time however all the affluent miners would have departed for their eternal journey leaving behind ruins of destruction and imminent environment holocaust to be faced by successive generations. What measures are being initiated on the ground to reclaim the exploited and barren coal and limestone mines? Whether any checks and balances exist to ensure adherence to environment norms in mining operations? Is the environment, ecological & social-economic impact assessment study, mandatory prior to actual mining and establishing an industry, being scrutinized to verify the ground reality and credibility of such exercise? What is the mechanism in place to ensure implementation of environment management plan? Our state is rich in bio resource including traditional and contemporary knowledge. The Biological Diversity Act, 2003 provides for constituting a State Biodiversity Board with the powers relating to the conservation of biodiversity, sustainable use of its components and equitable sharing of the benefits arising out of the utilization of biological resources. No positive steps have been taken in this direction as the epicenter of power till now was busy dispensing our inherent resources through the "single window" and accruing individual benefits through the "back door".

The Government has to accord serious thought on this vexed issue and act positively, before the situation reaches a point of no return. The traditional institutions, District Councils and civil society organizations will also have to put their act together and address the perilous issue which concerns the entire population of the state. This subject which is gradually coming into sharp focus will influence all future socio-economic and public interest interventions of the government.

4

Where has all the rain gone?

(Issue highlighted in the year 2007)

Bright sunshine, day temperature hovering around thirty degree centigrade, clear blue sky with nil rainfall. It is not the weather report of any city or town in the north or west of the country, but our own Shillong in the north east of India. The entire Shillong plateau is on the threshold of a noticeable deviation in climatic conditions. Although the phenomenon of "climate change" is yet to be conclusively established, "variation in climate" is being actually experienced all over the globe. In Shillong plateau, people are sweating out the unprecedented heat and unusual reduction in rainfall which is presently going through a deficit ranging from 40 to 65 percent, corresponding to normal precipitation during months of June and July respectively during previous years. This situation has undergone rapid changes in course of the last decade particularly after the Tsunami. I had expressed apprehension of similar rising temperature coupled with reduction in rainfall in and around Shillong plateau in coming years. Climate of a place is the average weather that is familiar over a period of time. The factors that determine the climate at a location are the rainfall, sunshine, wind, humidity, and temperature – all of which has been exhibiting a significant alteration for the worse. Such variations are dynamic, following a natural cycle and hence not easily noticeable. However, in our case the striking feature is that the transformation has been manifesting itself in matter of few years. Scientists are finding evidence of such changes from tree rings, pollen samples, ice cores, and sea sediments. Over the last 100 years the change has been rapid to which certain plant and animal species have found hard to adapt. However the shift in this region, particularly the declining rainfall pattern, has been marked since last few years.

Human induced activities are primarily responsible for the speed at which this change has occurred. It has acquired the potential to culminate into serious ecological aftermath. The causal factors are mainly the quantum leap in extraction and use of fossil fuels, destruction of forest and bio-diversity, increase in population with faulty land utilization, modern unplanned development, unscientific mining and quarrying, rising human and matching vehicle population etc. The atmosphere surrounding us has greenhouse gases of which carbon dioxide is the most harmful, released in large volumes due to above activities together with methane, nitrous oxide etc. The enhanced greenhouse effect is more commonly identified with triggering off global warming. Further, ozone layer has determined the temperature structure and safeguarded life on the planet by absorbing the harmful ultraviolet rays of the sun. But in the past half-century, humans have upset the delicate balance of nature and in the process destroying this life-protecting layer. The outcome is the increasingly common sight of gathering dark clouds in the Shillong skyline; being mostly incapable of precipitating or at most falling as light drizzle. The rain and moisture bearing clouds are evaporated due to high atmospheric temperature.

Emergence of a "Micro Climatic" zone is ostensibly in progression within Shillong plateau, reflected in the prevailing scenario of high temperature and low rainfall. Lack of precipitation due to increased atmospheric temperature and dissipation of rain or moisture bearing clouds is a common sight these days. The surrounding locales of Shillong are however experiencing near normal rainfall which further lend credence to a localized climatic variation, receiving few light drizzle at night when there is a fall in temperature when a modicum of precipitation is possible. This perceptible variation will adversely affect the population of the capital directly because of alterations in temperature and rainfall. A warmer climate within Shillong plateau is having direct impact on rainfall patterns and increase in the level of evaporation of surface water with threat of rise in the number of cyclones and hurricanes. This, in turn, will affect water resources, forests, and other natural ecological systems, power generation, infrastructure, and human health. Change in rainfall pattern is one of the most certain and imminent predictions of climate variation, closely followed by disruption of safe drinking water sources Ecosystems which sustain the earth's entire storehouse of species and genetic diversity are very sensitive to changes in climate. If the rate of climate inconsistency continues to accelerate, then the extinction of some plants and animals, endemic to our region is certain. The adverse effects have the potential to be catastrophic for Humankind. There is still a great deal that we do not understand about our climate, and about how our activities will change it. But one thing is clear – the process of reversing the human induced activities as highlighted above has to start in earnest or else it will probably be too late!

5

Let "Save Rivers" initiative begin from our home.

(Issue highlighted in the year 2012)

According to the old adage, charity begins at home. It still holds good to-day and "charity" includes initiation of deeds which are of common good. A home, household or family is where one often acquires important life values and habits and forms the foundation for other social and human organizations, including extent of their effectiveness and credibility. Thus, if all households and families within Shillong urban agglomerate become aware of the importance of not polluting the water bodies and take conscious efforts to reduce water pollution, it shall not take more than few years to rejuvenate both the streams and restore their past pristine glory within a decade. Water pollution solutions must first start with the household and the home. Preventing pollution of our waterways is everyone's responsibility. Our water bodies are suffering because of us; yet many say, "I don't contribute to the denigration". "How is it my problem?" It's everyone's problem and no matter where one lives within the catchment of Wah Umkhrah & Umshyrpi, can help save both these water bodies. At present there is no authority responsible for protection and conservation of rivers, streams in the State. The river front is everybody's concern, but what about the river itself. The Environment Protection Act 1986 provides adequate provisions for notifying a State Regulatory Authority for conservation of water sources including rivers, water bodies etc in addition to a Water Quality Assessment Authority. Besides lamenting, it is also imperative to look for solutions and arrest further deterioration.

Given the various causes of water pollution, there are many things that household can do to help with the water pollution problems locally. There is no doubt that governments and related public health and pollution control agencies have important roles to play in terms of how to stop water pollution, whether it is through education and awareness of the masses, or through putting in place proper and effective water cleaning and sewage systems, or through enforcing strict laws against water pollution by industries, households and individuals. Nonetheless, the responsibility for water pollution solutions does not only lie with the government and other statutory agencies. Households contribute significantly to water pollution by resorting to haphazard disposal of garbage, sewage and chemicals present in conventional cleaning liquids, garden pesticides, fertilizers et al. One of the best household water pollution solutions is to switch to household products which are usually biodegradable, and would break down into harmless substances after a while. As such, the impact they have on water sources and the environment is minimal. Although certain natural processes may cause some amount of water pollution, anthropogenic effects cause water pollution the most. We need to use water every day in our homes which comes from groundwater sources, rivers, and lakes. Most of the water we use and abuse finds its way back to one or more of the water bodies. The used water from agricultural and industrial practices, and household use, all comes together to generate sewage or wastewater. If sewage is allowed to flow back into water systems without being treated, it causes pollution. The polluted water bodies harm all life, humans, animal and plants. Water also gets polluted due to surface runoff which flow directly from household drains through storm-water drains into water bodies without any treatment. The disposal of sewage is a major problem in Shillong particularly direct discharge into the water bodies including the two streams thus carrying disease causing bacteria and viruses into sources of water. While we should see to it that the government is stringent about their policies related to sewage treatment plants and methods, there are many things that we can carry out individually to prevent water pollution.

Everyday household activities are a major contributor to polluted runoff, which is among the most serious sources of water contamination. When it rains, different household pollutants are all washed into storm water drains and sewers to discharge into the one of the two streams which finally flows down and empties into the "endangered" Umiam Lake – a virtual septic tank of 10 sq kms area burdened with multifarious ecological impingement generated over 220 sq kms of its catchment area. These are the same lakes, rivers and streams we rely on for drinking, bathing, swimming and fishing. Some ways to reduce polluted household runoff includes proper disposal of solid waste (garbage) and hazardous waste. Installation of low cost garbage traps at the outlet of drains and recycling of household sullage prior to discharge in addition to "rain garden" which capture runoff in shallow depressions and allows it to soak into the ground, instead of running off to the storm drains. This process not only serves as water pollution solutions, it also helps to replenish underground water with water filtered by the soil. Reducing use of water is one of the easy-to-implement water pollution solutions. Less water used means less water polluted thereby treated before it gets discharged since over 70% of the water used in our home is either flushed down the toilet or shower drain. Impervious surfaces around our home must be minimized. Septic tank requires timely cleaning as effluent from failed or poorly maintained septic systems can contaminate groundwater or seep into storm water drains.

Once an individual household is no longer a source of pollution, community action to improve one's immediate neighbourhood followed by the locality becomes easier to implement. Rejuvenation of rivers and all forms of water bodies has to be a sustained people's movement which may take even a decade or more to educe results on the ground. The people's movement to restore and conserve our water bodies is imperative through a public awareness and sensitization, particularly of the young children and student community. This young demographic asset, is the hope to reverse the damage caused by elders. It is time for Shillongites, particularly the youth to rise to the occasion and show the world that we can do it together and make it happen – pollution free and clean rivers and streams.

6

Water conservation Or Dry and barren future.

(Issue highlighted in the year 2006)

One of the early lessons a child learns in school, is that water covers 70% of Earth's surface and only 30 percent comprises of land, out of which around 15 percent can support life. Yet in a couple of year's time, the child is perplexed at the dichotomy of ground reality - water scarcity. It is ironical but true. This grim veracity has become a cause of concern all over the globe. The situation in our country too is extremely depressing. India is among the countries that will be worst hit by water scarcity in the new millennium and is expected to encounter severe water stress by 2020. It is estimated that almost 100 million people faces drought conditions, reflecting ominous portent of a dry and barren future. The north eastern region of the country, particularly the hills are perilously poised although it may not be apparent from the prevailing situation. It will not take long compared to the plains, for the situation to take an abrupt turn for the worst. The severe water crisis at Sohra (Cherrapunjee) especially during dry months, in spite of being one of the highest rainfall locales in the world, is definitely a forewarning of the approaching danger. Mizoram is another state which is in the threshold of severe water stress. Similarly, there are innumerable such indications especially in densely populated areas, spread throughout the region, including state capitals like Shillong, Aizawl and Itanagar, emanating such definite warning signal.

In the north east, problem of water crisis gaining momentum, in spite of high rainfall, can primarily be attributed to rapid decline in the fragile resource base due to various anthropogenic activities. This has finally led to degradation and loss of forest cover including the areas comprising the catchments. The gradual shrinking of this invaluable natural resource is impinging directly on the ecological stability, biological diversity, and environmental security of the region in general and catchments in particular, which are natures indigenous "water reservoirs". These "store houses" have been exposed to over exploitation on account of increase in population, associated with deforestation for commercial felling, diverse land use pattern, pastoral and agronomic activities, shifting cultivation, modern unplanned development and unscientific mining and quarrying.

Further no organized water management regime has ever been followed, for which there is haphazard movement of water instead of proper seepage and percolation and increase of supply to the natural "stores". It is a common human psychology that whatever is available free to us is neglected and defiled, particularly the resource(s) bestowed by nature. Water requires no harnessing or generation as in case of other non-renewable sources like power, timber, fossil fuel and mineral deposits where financial liability is mandatory to the consumer. The ecology movement since 1960's onwards has postulated the theory that people must cultivate the habit to live, within the limitations of Earth's infinite supply of resources. The countries which adopted the philosophy and initiated preventive measures and scrupulously maintaining them are to-day better insulated from the danger. That the situation is not yet beyond salvage in the north east is mainly due to factors like high rainfall, small population and just enough forest cover to retain and store water. It is evident from records, that neither Sahara, Thar nor any of the deserts were originally in their present state. There was presence of sufficient forest cover in those areas. The degradation of ecological equilibrium, led to the evolution of desert conditions which manifest now. The rapidly receding forest cover in the north eastern states is primarily responsible for water stress. A study conducted in Sohra (Cherrapunjee) – *the wettest place on earth* and adjoining areas confirmed our apprehension, that it is not a question of non-availability of water but a consequence of unplanned use and misuse of natural resources coupled with total ignorance and lack of initiative to conserve water, resulting in bulk of the rain water flowing down the hilly terrain into the plains. There is hardly any effort to conserve this valuable component, required on a sustained basis in perpetuity to sustain life.

It is a matter of concern, whether to consider water as a renewable resource or a non - renewable component of nature. In fact as per situation prevailing in our country, water can at best be classified as renewable, if subjected to recycling and adoption of proper management techniques for conservation. Delay will render this vital daily requirement for survival next only to oxygen, to be relegated to non renewable status and consequently endangering the sustenance of all forms of life in planet Earth. The time is ripe to revert back to nature and be guided by its numerous inherent mechanisms. Nature has its own ingenious way of purifying and recycling water. The phenomenon of evaporation, condensation and precipitation – another primary level School lesson for a child, serves to confirm with clarity, nature's original system of maintaining equilibrium. The lack of water recycling and careful management will invariably lead to water stress, and eventually becoming a non renewable source as far as the hills are concerned. Accordingly all the water allowed to flow down is forever lost and not a drop which has either accumulated in the Brahmaputra or the Bay of Bengal will be of any help to retrieve the crisis.

A concerted and sincere effort is essential to evolve a partnership through networking, between water related industries, government, municipalities, NGOs, research and educational institutions, and above all communities. This will open avenues for funding, technical assistance, synergistic and lateral thinking for innovative solutions, and increased public awareness, for integrated management of water resources based on the following:-

- In view of ecological degradation of majority catchments in the north east, it is imperative to undertake intensive management which will include enacting laws to ensure total ban on felling of trees, shifting cultivation, opening of land, quarrying and mining in the catchments, irrespective of ownership and status of land. Environmental damage in India, it is reckoned reduces GDP by 10 per cent annually, which is equivalent to around $ 40 billion.

- At the same time, massive afforestation measures will have to form the focal point of treatment, and all degraded and vacant areas of catchments brought under tree cover, with simultaneous establishment of major engineering structures and undertaking minor soil conservation measures.

- Watershed development to bring the degraded, unproductive land under tree cover. It would cost hundreds of crores to construct water storage equivalent to what even the existing forests of north east store. In terms of water storage, check of soil erosion etc, the value of such forests in monetary terms would be much more than the total value of all industrial assets and non renewable sources of energy.

- Water Recycle is an effective and economical way of solving water scarcity. Recycle of effluents, domestic sullage and sewage not only conserve vast volumes of water, but also protects the environment by reducing pollution.

- Reviving the traditional rain water storage systems that existed in most villages and composting bio toilets to reduce water use.

- The supply to aquifers particularly in the hilly terrain has to be canalized and enhanced including strengthening of such natural storage structures to increase their water holding and carrying capacity.

- The proliferation of energized wells has to be restricted, since such wells have depleted ground water all over the country ranging from 1 to 3 meters a year depending on their location. Such wells can be allowed, if matching replenishment measures are ensured. Over extraction of ground water has led to intrusion of polluted water into aquifers, resulting in problems of excess iron and fluoride as evident in Karbi Anglong region of Assam).

Thus the immediate priority will be to draw an Action Plan for Water sanctuaries and creating associated infrastructure for providing water security for sustainable development, based on following parameters, to begin with.

- Urban Initiatives:-

  o Encourage public involvement in privatization of civic utilities and services on the basis of smaller systems, designed ward wise.

  o Building codes should make it compulsory for rain water harvesting and water recycling.

o Felling of trees, quarrying and mining in and around urban locales, should be banned by law.

- Rural Agenda:-

  o Training in water conservation measures and selecting specific schemes for implementation.

  o Technology adapted to rural needs.

  o Use of information technology for education and awareness.

  o Coordinate with companies and industrial houses, either located in the north east or marketing their products in this region, to set up rural marketing division to support NGOs in training local youth to operate and maintain various equipment, plant & machineries used in management of water for agriculture, irrigation and drinking. This will be of immense help to the rural communities for implementation of various innovative schemes which envisages direct

> funding to rural communities for execution of water supply projects on technical guidance and monitoring.
>
> o   Feedback from field to technology.

- Funding and Allocation:-

Several hundreds of crores are available annually to fund projects, like Watershed Development, much of it funded by the World Bank, Asian Development Bank and international funding agencies and individual countries. At present it is all routed through the Union Government to different states and used by government departments. The time has come to review such unproductive expenditure and a truly representative and responsible state level body constituted, representing government, reputable companies, well known NGOs with proven track record, resource persons, sufficient number of women members and educational institutions. This body will allocate funds only to projects capable of executing time-bound programmes and reporting with total transparency to the public periodically on physical and financial achievement.

I would like to conclude with a relevant verse, based on Bob Dylan's famous song "Blowin' in the Wind", as visualized by Shankar Ranganathan, a dedicated exponent of water conservation & treatment infrastructure in India.

How many years will our forest exist
Before they end up in smoke?
How many years will our people exist
if they think the forest's a joke?
Listen. How many crops will a desert produce?
And how much water to drink?
The answer, my friend, is blowin'
in the wind
The answer is blowin' in the wind.

7

Nature's fury, man's agony.

(Issue highlighted in the year 2004)

The fury of flood wreck havoc in the plains of India and foothills of the north east region of the country, during monsoon. At the same time, prolonged dry spell desiccate large tracts in the west of the country, activating drought conditions all over. The rage of flash floods and cloud burst do not remain a mute spectator, in all this devastation. Hundreds of life and dwelling houses are destroyed and families displaced from their roots. It is a reprehensible defeat for Man. His negligence, self-righteousness and greed are the sole reason for countless heartbreaking tragedies. All these calamities are warning signals to slow down the pace of denigrating and defying nature and return to nature's realm. The only irony and aberration is that innocent lives are made to compensate for our acts of omission and failings. Nature also appears to have been influenced by the diversity of the prevailing system. There is inflow of plenty where there is excess and a trickle where there is little. The simultaneous occurrence of flood and drought in areas where it is least wanted, punctuated by other natural calamities; reflect the symptom of this trend. Today it is one locale; tomorrow it may be another other city, town or village. It is only during a calamity in one's backyard when the reverie is broken – albeit for a short duration.

Disaster when it strikes whether in the air, land or water usually results in human tragedy. Ironically, most of these disasters cannot be prevented. However, a number of them can be easily averted with little foresight, rational planning and restraining human greed for commercial gains. It should perfectly be possible to insulate people from the worst effects of a disaster by taking preventive measures through an effective disaster management strategy. In almost all cases, the extent of human suffering can be reduced through timely help, sensitivity of the management team and above all basic awareness of people who have become the victims. All disaster management policy should be formulated on the concept of reducing both the risk of incidence and after affect of disaster. The speed of response to any disaster particularly floods, which is an annual feature in the northeast of India, depends completely on the level of preparedness of the concerned authorities and the sensitivity of the people. It would be nearly impossible to face any such calamitous situation without local support.

Most disasters, like flooding, affect members of vulnerable low income groups more disproportionately, resulting in more killings and injuries than relatively developed areas. This particular segment of society cannot afford to live in safe zones nor protect them effectively. Recurrent floods may result in fatalistic behaviour and resignation of the vulnerable people, which will compound the problems when it comes to protect them effectively. They appear to have resigned to their fate of facing nature's fury year after year. An increasingly urbanized world holds the potential to assist much greater number of people affected by disasters owing to its superior responsiveness, while the civic authorities' abilities on this front can be greatly enhanced through effective and accountable governance.

North East is not insulated from occurrence of such distressing tragedy, engulfing the most vulnerable and hapless. Most of the State capitals and other small towns fall within the seismic fault line. This is in addition to the frequency of floods causing intense devastation in the region. Natural disasters can have a life-altering impact on the individuals, families and society and the effect can be felt at the community, city and state level, or many times can impact an entire country. How well the impact of a disaster event is absorbed has much to do with the intensity of the impact and the level of preparedness and resilience. Just as a natural phenomenon can change the landscape of our personal lives as well as aspects of our community, so too can different types of disasters drastically alter the natural environment. Environmental conditions may aggravate the impact of a disaster or conversely have an impact on the environment. Deforestation, forest management practices, agriculture systems etc. can worsen the negative environmental impacts of a storm or typhoon, leading to landslides, flooding, silting, ground and surface water contamination. The interaction of disasters and environment has both short-term and long-term effects affecting people, ecosystem and bio-diversity. Poorer environmental conditions such as diminished biodiversity, soil degradation or growing food scarcity can easily threaten food security for people dependent on the products of land, forests, pastures and marine environment for their livelihoods. As natural resources become scarcer, the range of options available to communities become more limited, reducing the availability of coping solutions and reducing local resilience to hazards or capacity to recover from disasters. Over a period of time, environmental factors can further increase vulnerability by creating new and undesirable patterns of social discord, economic destitution and eventually forced migration of entire communities.

Around the globe, land use and land cover changes are eroding the natural buffers that protect communities from hazard risk. There is a need to highlight the role that comprehensive environmental management can play in reducing the risk of disasters, and to mitigate the consequences - both on human lives and on the broader ecology. We also need to explore the link between environmental systems and disasters, and also the synergies between man-made and natural disasters. The increasing frequency and severity of man-made and natural disasters may well be changing the global environment. All of these threats to the environment have been apparent in recent disasters. Mitigating the effects of disasters are primary components in global efforts to ensure environmental security.

It is time for all to take a break, introspect and initiate positive steps to erase even the minimum of scope for such calamity overtaking us. The least, which we can do, is to ensure the safety of our children, who optimistically will not be complacent and indifferent citizens like most of us.

8

Mining on sustained yield principle.

(Issue highlighted in the year 2007)

An interesting debate in the state of Meghalaya was pertaining to mining "within" & "outside" forest land and status of items like limestone available therein which was referred to as "minor" forest produce, as per Indian Forest Act, 1927; Section 4(b)(iv). However, this definition is not the final word. Subsequent amendment with enactment of Forest (Conservation) Act 1980 with amendments in 1988 & 2006 was to deal with changing times to help conserve and manage the country's forest better. The question in context of our state is classifying "within" and "outside" forest area. There is no third category of classification as meaning of word forest has been clearly defined.

The Supreme Court's involvement in forest conservation largely centres on the Public Interest Litigation viz *T. N Godavarman Thirumulpad Vs Union of India (W.P 202 of 1995)*. In the same order the court clarified that the word 'forest' must be understood according to the dictionary meaning of the term irrespective of the nature of ownership and classification thereof. This led to fundamental changes that have wide impact on forest management. Prior to it the word 'forest' was limited only to government declared forests irrespective of whether it had tree cover or not. Likewise, areas with significant tree cover were not regarded as 'forest' simply because in government records it was not declared as 'forest'. Due to this, large areas under good forest cover were outside the purview of the Forest(Conservation) Act, 1980. The court's clarification expanded statutory recognition to forests, irrespective of nature of ownership and classification. This implies that forests could be designated as reserved and protected whether they are privately owned or otherwise under the Forest (Conservation) Act, section 2(1). Less than two years after the first order in the Godavarman case, was another one in 1998, where the court directed that working plans for all forest divisions shall be prepared by the state governments and would have to be approved by the central government. It was clarified that the term 'State Government' would also include District Councils constituted

under Schedule VI of the Constitution of India.
Most Autonomous District Councils in our state
are either preparing or incorporating changes
recommended by approving authority in the
working or management plan of forest falling
within their respective jurisdiction. Thus, for
argument sake it can be said that technically all
land, water bodies etc under control of the three
district councils are forest, pending categorization
and approval of working plans. Consequently,
NOC etc in matters of forest has to be based on
approved working plan.

The 1998 order met with stiff criticism in the
north east, on the grounds that the court was
making an arbitrary directive which had not taken
into account the special constitutional provisions
for the region. More importantly, it was felt that
the order had failed to appreciate the traditional
management systems of tribal communities. These
orders were seen as being aimed at reinforcing
centralized power structures. Implementation of
the court's orders on prohibiting logging without
an approved working plan led to some adverse
consequences on rural economy in Meghalaya.
Commercial sale of timber was carried on by
large number of farmer families being the only

source to sustain their livelihood. The biggest impact of the ban has been in the use of trees. Since trees lost sale value as timber, farmers turned to harvest trees for usage of lower value, being sold for one tenth the price as firewood, on the sale of which there is no ban on being classed as minor forest produce. Making charcoal from burning cut logs and tree branches, which had virtually disappeared, resurfaced in the new millennium with a vengeance. Small farmers preferred to convert forested lands into agricultural plots or were forced to sell their land to wealthy individuals. The process is going on at the peril of rural inhabitants. Wood based industries could foresee the decline and started looking for fresh ventures which started with ferro-alloys and diversified into cement, based on potential of the huge limestone deposit in the state. And from environment point of view scientific extraction of limestone at the right areas on a limited scale is any time better than clear felling of forest areas. Investments in the sector, with establishment of few plants were definitely heartening for the economy especially after the ban on timber trade. However, with passage of time a mad rush for cement plants was witnessed without a realistic evaluation of the limestone reserve and their location within or outside forest areas. There is no concrete plan for utilizing the limestone reserve on a sustained basis in perpetuity. On the contrary, the popular fable of the fate that ensues to the hen laying the golden egg is clearly evident. The Forest Act 2006 emphasizes on non-destructive harvesting on the basis of sustained yield principle, as prescribed in the working plan and maximum quantity of the minor forest produce that can be harvested from any forest land (s). It has been recognised at the national level that the collection, processing and trade in minor forest produce should be endowed with the forest dependent communities on the principle of 'share and care'.

In order to strike a realistic balance between industrial growth, beneficial to maximum possible members of the indigenous community and protection of environment is imperative. To-day the benefits are reaped by a handful. In order to achieve this, a comprehensive action plan is required, conforming to legal guidelines and not resorting to subverting environment and other related norms. Such an approach shall sooner than later lead to another possible ban like that of timber. Instead of avoiding and concealing issues on the ground, modification and clarifications of orders and directives can be easily sought by filing intervention applications. There have been many instances where modifications were made in order to deal with specific situations. Similar interventions could help address conservation needs and economic growth. Biodiversity conservation and livelihood rights are critical for the ecological and social security. Today, judicial intervention in forest matters is a reality. The environment bench of Supreme Court has been taking a proactive role in passing orders that impact forest governance. While this may not be an ideal situation, it is a reality. The development trends in the country today are at the cost of the environment because of disregard for environmental laws. Citizens have asked the Supreme Court repeatedly to intervene because 'private' interests have attempted to bypass laws. Clearances required under the Forest Conservation Act or the Environment Protection Act, are often simply not taken. As a result legal intervention is sought. It is not a question of technicalities on status of the land but the entire biodiversity and evolving equilibrium between conservation and economic activity, primarily beneficial to majority of the indigenous community.

9

Sharing spoils of mining.

(Issue highlighted in the year 2009)

The draft of the State Mining Policy which has been in the public domain for over a year is yet to be given a final shape. There are many grey areas which need to be sorted before finalizing the draft, like clarity on mining "within or outside forest areas" being foremost. Further, consensus on every section of the policy is most unlikely since absolute authority and freedom enjoyed by individual miners and mine owners on nature and mode of mining shall be curbed together with provision for protection of the eco-system. Scientific mining and environment protection measures including mine safety infrastructure entail additional expenditure, which most miners shall resist. However, the delay maybe a blessing in disguise for the common man residing in mining areas. A bill that promises direct benefit to people from the minerals underneath their land requires mining companies to shell out a portion of their profit for people displaced or affected by their operations. The bill would replace the existing Mines and Minerals Development and Regulation (MMDR) Act of 1957. The profit-sharing provision requires mining including coal companies to share their net profit every year with the affected communities. Companies that mine major minerals like limestone and iron ore will have to give the affected people an amount equal to the royalty that they pay to the state government annually. For those mining minor minerals like sandstone and marble, the states will decide the profit-sharing percentage in consultation with the proposed National Mining Regulatory Authority. It is essential for mining companies to pay a percentage of their annual profit or 100 per cent of the royalty, whichever is higher, to communities. This would not apply to the nationalized coal sector, which would pay 26 per cent of the profit. In Meghalaya the situation is complex and the mining policy can only address the issue to factor in the salient features of MMDR Bill. The same may not be applicable to coal mines particularly, which escaped nationalization and individual mine owners have absolute rights over the coal extracted from their individual mines including pricing etc except for paying a small royalty to the government. This is the first time the concept of natural resource rent is being established in the country.

In this age of green accounting, the wealth of the nation in terms of its value to equity and sustainability is gaining priority. Green growth is fundamentally about inclusive growth. The proposed Meghalaya Mining Policy can factor in the essence of the bill and make it mandatory for coal miners and in case of other minerals like limestone, the manufacturer / company utilizing the minerals as raw materials to produce an end product to pay a fixed amount to the community inhabiting the mining areas. This will ensure sustainable development of the people and environment, both of which are suffering due to mining, including those displaced or affected by such operations. The approach of the policy has to be sustainable development of people and not sustainable development of mining. The fund so generated can be utilized for example in amelioration of ground water and treating highly contaminated water run-off from mines due to high sulphur content in coal mining areas of north east. Treatment of abandoned mines and adverse affect on agricultural land is another sector which requires immediate attention to avoid a looming environment catastrophe. Apart from greenhouse gas emissions the fact of the matter is that in India mining has led to large-scale degradation of the environment.

Mining cannot be stopped or wished away however hard one tries. Then there are various economic considerations and utilization of minerals for production of end product like cement for example. The best out of a worst situation is to strike a realistic balance between industrial growths, mining and accrual of maximum possible benefit to the State and its people with priority on protection of environment. To-day the benefits are reaped by a handful, whether from mining minerals or exploiting industrial/ transport subsidy. In order to broad base the benefits, after attaining equilibrium, is to set up effective district level units, both for collection and utilization of the funds for the people; generated from miners/mining companies, with priority and need based strategies and interventions. The common men should get their share from the natural resource like minerals. The mining policy must give preference to tribal cooperatives for mining small deposits. A detailed mining plan needs to be submitted even by individual miners highlighting the scientific approach, environment protection measures, infrastructure to treat contaminated water emerging from mines, afforestation initiatives particularly over abandoned mines. In addition, it is important to evaluate the gross available stock of minerals and regulate the annual exploitation commensurate to protection and conservation measures. To ensure transparency in the system, the policy has to ensure mining companies to put all data related to grant, extension, termination and plan of operations in the public domain. That mining companies do not follow eco friendly practices is quite evident because six to nine hectares of land is destroyed for every one million tonnes of mineral produced. Mineworkers' safety also seems to be a low-priority subject for the industry since there are 30-non-fatal but disabling accidents per tonne of mineral produced, and one death per 2.5 tonnes. The situation in Meghalaya could be worse. A realistic appraisal is necessary and findings of the study have to form a base for undertaking suitable reforms measure.

10

Spare the pine trees; use the pine needles.

(Issue highlighted in the year 2010)

The felling and conversion of mature trees, mainly conifers, into charcoal is an added cause for decline of forest cover in the state of Meghalaya and other eastern Himalayan states. In the early days, charcoal was produced in a limited manner for domestic use in high altitude areas where normal coal reserves were not available. However, with the mushrooming growth of ferro alloy units in the state, in the early years of the millennium, production of charcoal gained momentum. Charcoal is an important raw material component for ferro alloy units and consequently large scale commercial production of the same began with clear felling high forest, extending to hundreds of hectares. The consumption is not restricted to ferro alloys and other industries. Domestic consumption of charcoal is on the upswing due to rising cost of energy and fuel sources like LPG and kerosene. A school of thought attributes the indulgence of charcoal production as a source of livelihood after the Apex court ban on felling of trees, irrespective of ownership and status of such forests. This logic cannot be an excuse for rampant clear felling of forest. If trees are to be felled to provide livelihood then why ban the functioning of saw and veneer mills? This sector too was providing livelihood to thousands before the Supreme Court ban on felling of trees. The concern must be to develop an alternate source of energy and fuel to meet the industrial and domestic demand; which in turn shall also take care of livelihood issue. Innovative approach has given results in other areas of the country. Converting organic waste material into briquettes for heating and cooking is a big success like pyrolisation of sugar cane leaves into charcoal dust. The integrated fuel-from-waste system can create thousands of rural entrepreneurs, while saving trees and reducing petro dependence. Charcoal from coconut shell is used widely as domestic and industrial fuel. Charcoal made from bamboo finds ready uses and markets. The high density of bamboo growing stock in Meghalaya can be converted in specially designed brick kilns, developed and tested by the National Mission on Bamboo Applications (NMBA), to make quality

charcoal in an efficient, safe and reliable manner.
Moreover, large scale plantation of bamboo, which
is a short rotation crop, can also be undertaken for
conversion into charcoal.

The goal should be to transform the current
charcoal industry from a necessary evil to a
rewarding opportunity for thousands of people.
This can be achieved by replacing the source of
charcoal from trees to an alternate prospective
source - forest floor and fields. In Khasi Jaintia
hills region of Meghalaya, one witnesses regular
forest fires during dry season particularly severe in
pine forests. Lakhs of tons of biomass is generated
from forest residues mainly pine needles. It is
imperative to remove the needles from the forest
floor due to their high inflammable nature. A
pine tree trunk is heat resistant and can survive
fire of such nature but in the process destroy
both regeneration and growth of other plant
species including micro organisms. Dry pine
foliage also stops water absorption by the soil and
sunlight from reaching the ground. However,
the negative characteristics can be converted
into constructive and positive virtue if utilized
judiciously. In the Garhwal region of Uttarakhand
pine needles – above 60% in ratio, mixed with

other forest produce and agricultural wastes are used in manufacturing of biomass briquettes. This raw material is briquetted to a density of around 650 per cubic metre where around 1.3 kg of briquette replace 1 kg of charcoal. The initiative has to be taken by both the Forest & Environment Department and KHADC under one of the numerous schemes of MoEF for minor forest produce. Women Self Help Groups both in urban and rural areas with specific jurisdiction can be set up for collection of the needles and other forest residues and agricultural waste. The briquette processing unit on a pilot project mode with installed capacity of 20,000 tonnes per annum will have to be established preferably in the private sector with capital investment of about Rs 2.5 crores. Subsidy and other benefits now guzzled by environment denigrating industries can also be made available to an environment benign intervention in addition to sale of carbon credits generated by the project to any one of the numerous international agencies. Moreover, the project shall at one end save the forest from being sacrificed for charcoal production and at the other end empower economically weaker section with the double benefit of an alternative source of livelihood and "green" energy resource.

Pinus kesiya which bears the brunt of being sacrificed for converting into charcoal is in the IUCN red list of threatened species. A recent phenomenon observed in the pine forest. A prominent brown wide horizontal streak, extending for quite a distance has appeared in the mid section of this forest area and can distinctly noticeable even from far. The extended band of brown in monsoon drew our attention. Preliminary investigation over an accessible strip, part of the comprehensive "brown crown" belt, reveals that foliage or needles in the canopy of most pine (Pinus kesiya) trees have turned brown – an occurrence common in winter. One reason could be that in this species, needles are formed in three flushes during a year. And the dryness precedes emergence of a new flush in the offing. Seasonality in birth and death of needles is an important adaptive strategy which determines the formation of a true canopy. But the intrigue is how all trees of varying age group in a particular stretch are exhibiting such top drying. Experts need to undertake scientific study on priority. Does the phenomenon reflect "winter for Pinus kesiya in spring". It will be a tragedy of great consequence if the coming generation has to fall back on photo albums and archives to find out what a conifer like Pinus kesiya tree looked like.

11

Methodical & eco-friendly urban planning.

(Issue highlighted in the year 2006)

The North Eastern States, particularly Assam has been able to harness substantial foreign funds over the years, for undertaking developmental projects. Such finances have come either as soft loans, loan-cum grant or grant-in aid from sources like World Bank, ADB, OECF or individual nations. One such innovative project is the initiative of the Australian government aimed at developing the civic amenities in Shillong and Gangtok. The entire project termed as "Aus-aid", has been funded by Australia with focus on improving and streamlining the functioning of civic amenities like water supply, sanitation, solid waste management, and sewage treatment in the two state capitals. This particular project has been introduced with a basic difference in mode of implementation. While in most of the foreign aided ventures, fund is released by the concerned financial institution, organization or country to the beneficiary states for execution of approved projects. Whereas, in this particular case the Australian Government, instead of releasing funds directly to Meghalaya and Sikkim, appointed an internationally renowned firm-Kellog's Brown & Root (KBR) Pty. Ltd in the year 2004, to implement the multifarious component of the schemes, earmarked for the two state capitals. Initially there has been intense speculation regarding actual agenda of proposed action plan and their viability as far as Shillong is concerned. In absence of comprehensive information and lack of understanding pertaining to whatever little details of the project was available; emission of doubts was a natural corollary. Silence and low profile of the Aus- Aid Team preceded by the slow pace in getting off the "starting block" added to the unease. The Government too could not clarify with clarity, resulting in avoidable misconception and confusion. As lot of fanfare like laying of foundation stone etc of such projects, is mandatory with our system, the absence of similar display in this venture, must have caught all by surprise and added momentum to misgiving encompassing the project. Interestingly, during this period (as evident now) of deliberation and doubt the Aus- Aid Team had already embarked in their mission and was busy laying the foundation, albeit of a different nature- a tangible urban planning module, particularly formulation of GIS, pertaining to almost all civic components of Shillong and Gangtok.

The public expression of apprehension regarding veracity of schemes and a question mark on their efficacy must have been one of the plausible reasons for curtailment of the Project size and duration. The Aus-Aid Team must have realized the hard way that silence is not always golden, in our method of working. In spite of a muted approach, information regarding the multifarious projects initiated by Aus- Aid filtered out into public domain. An estimated 27 small grant and couple of demonstration schemes have already been established in different localities of Shillong. Aus Aid bears 70% of the total cost of approved project while the beneficiary (community) is liable to contribute the balance 30%. The demonstration projects fully funded by Aus –Aid, highlight modern concepts in positioning of water pipe lines, uniform distribution of water, installation of water meter, establishing sewage treatment and re-cycling mechanism, garbage collection and disposal, improved sanitation and drainage. The idea is to replicate such innovative projects in other areas of the two capitals, subject to their success and acceptability. The KBR group, responsible for implementing the project is not inclined to publicize their intervention before ensuring cent percent success rate, conforming to specific quality and efficiency standardized for each scheme. However, the most important mission of Aus- Aid appears to be the formulation of the GIS or Geographical Information System for both the locales.

The use of GIS in infrastructure development is a recent experience in India. Yet this system is being increasingly used in different sectors ranging from telecom and power to designing of township and municipal network. The impetus has come from IT and rising investment in infrastructure improvement. Shillong is among the few urban locales in the country and the first in North East besides Gangtok, where a comprehensive urban GIS application is being developed by Aus- Aid Team. This application is an essential decision support system for any local urban or civic authority involved in road, solid & bio medical waste management, sanitation & drainage, sewage treatment including property tax assessment and collection. There are basically three steps in formulating such GIS. The vital first phase involves study of available data with local authorities and their utilization. The data can be collected from three different sources-satellite images, aerial photos and ground survey. A judicious combination of all three is the ideal solution for India. This is followed by the most time and money consuming phase of analyzing and collecting new data, their assessment and mapping. The third phase involves implementation stage like application development, customization and training.

A GIS model for Shillong will primarily have a scientifically prepared digital base map at the macro plane, highlighting the existing infrastructure facilities like roads, drains including footpath, water bodies and network of pipelines, built-up areas etc encompassing all municipal areas. At the micro level, detailed digital maps will be drawn up reflecting property, buildings and other utilities. These digital maps have been constructed, based on data available with PHED, SMB & Urban Affairs Department, besides collection of inputs at the ground level by Aus-Aid Consultants. These digital maps, in spite of technical ability, are not affordable to majority of civic authorities in view of the prohibitive cost. In case of Shillong, this vital database is being made affordable by the Aus- Aid intervention. Shillong and its adjoining localities, which together can be termed as Greater Shillong, has been divided in consonance with existing Dorbar and Municipal Ward to facilitate execution of schemes in an organized manner. Moreover, the urban areas have been segregated into 7 "townships"- Shillong Municipal Board, Cantonment, Madanriting, Mawlai, Nongmynsong, Nongthymmai and Pynthorumkhrah. These demarcations will each form a particular administrative block for the purpose of proper governance and improving the financial health of civic authorities, particularly Shillong Municipal Board. The intensive exercise, involving property enumeration and mapping using GIS as a tool, is said to be in progress. All information pertaining to a property like location, year of construction, floor, covered and total area including infrastructural information such as water, sewer and electricity connection is being collected. This will help in removing the gap between assessed and non evaluated records while providing an opportunity for reassessment of properties. Finally, there is a proposal to computerize the entire billing system, to eliminate the dynamics of revenue "leakage" mechanism, similar to leaking water pipes. The resultant increase in revenue accruing from this exercise will be enormous, leading to financial stability of the Municipal Board.

The Aus– Aid exercise if carried to a logical conclusion will have put in place a viable and streamlined civic delivery system to resolve most civic issues and problems. What remains unresolved is the apprehensions of sceptics, particularly in Shillong, like "What happens when Aus Aid Team, finally pack up and the present CEO move out of SMB?" The question, though hypothetical is not totally unfounded since the entire exercise is not a onetime operation but involves the onerous task of replicating the "models" developed by Aus– Aid over the entire project area. Moreover, training of staff, regular survey, updating of data is imperative for survival of the system. There is no room for guesswork as time only will reveal whether a sound functional structure could be built on the foundation created by the Aus– Aid intervention. In the meantime, the least which New Delhi can do is to restore the original period of the project, if the initiative achieves its prime objective of installing a full proof infrastructure for all civic amenities in Shillong and Gangtok. And why not make efforts to bring other state capitals of the region to experience the Aus- aid intervention?

12

Monsoon mayhem and waste management.

(Issue highlighted in the year 2009)

Monsoon is associated with muck, filth, flooding and stench. Shillong which was an exception not too long ago is fast becoming like most other cities & towns. A light shower is sufficient to liberate the debris hitherto hidden in drains or occupying the streams, out into the open. As the downpour eases most roads and lanes look as if it was raining plastics & garbage. In some localities, faecal matter from open defecation floats along. Flooding of low lying areas due to spill over from trash clogged streams & drains are a common annual feature. The ground is prepared for the assorted strain of virus, bacteria and other pathogens to establish and attack with impunity. Water borne diseases are the most prominent, gaining entry to leaking and damaged network of pipelines. Most human ailment is the outcome of water- borne diseases. The root cause of this chaos is haphazard and disorganized disposal of solid waste generated at source. It is necessary to act positively and strike at the roots instead of reactive measures. The focus should shift to the source of waste generation to regulate and control this menace. Both social isolation and penal action must be initiated against open dumping of solid waste. Segregation and collection of garbage at source is not nuclear science but a matter of developing a habit. The process of reviving the past glory of our capital should start from our home, locality, workplace including commercial establishments, institutions et al. Although easier said than done the old adage prevention being better still holds good. And coming to cure, hospitals and nursing homes which are meant to restore health may also be responsible in spreading sickness unwittingly or as a smart "business strategy". The drains in the vicinity of most hospitals reveal open dumping of solid and hospital waste including disposables. The Bio Medical Waste (Management & Handling) Rules which stipulates 5 broad category of treatment process is either adhered to partially or not followed at all nor monitored and invoked by concerned authority. It appears as if anything and everything emanating from a hospital is curative in nature! The wholesale market and commercial zones account for a major chunk of abandoning litter. Most hotels and restaurants are also responsible for open dumping of garbage and waste. An inhospitable exercise resorted to by the hospitality sector!

Environment restorative activities like treatment of sewage, bio-medical waste and solid waste is a new concept. The need for such exercise was not felt necessary in the hills, primarily due to the terrain and low population density and cleanliness being an innate nature of the indigenous people. Gravity and vast stretches of available land was allowed to take care of such issues in a natural way. However, the ground situation has undergone rapid changes over the last few decades. This transformation has been brought about by change in demographic profile, migration and increase in population with proportionate generation of waste leading to random dumping of garbage, faulty disposal of sewage and other wastes.

Shillong is fortunate in having the first and the only solid waste composting plant in the North East. Yet the menace of solid waste is on the increase. The area of attention is to enforce separation at source, regular collection mechanism and timely transportation to the plant for disposal. Among the few early initiatives on Public Private

Participation (PPP) in urban infrastructure in this region, this plant having an installed capacity to treat and dispose 100 tonnes of solid waste per day, had once closed the chapter of open dumping of garbage in the gorges and valleys. This compost plant was a centre of motivation for other states in the region to emulate. Another hallmark of this plant was not allowing even the waste to go waste. It has the capacity to produce 15 tonnes of organic manure daily from the treated garbage. This low cost soil rejuvenator is finding wide acceptability and a boon for farmers in the State. The plant can be upgraded through introduction of latest technology for conversion of solid waste to "green" energy generation and above all installing a plastic & paper re-cycling plant on priority. This shall minimize the amount of material land filled. The plant with multifarious benefits, both existing and potential is explicatory "garbage to gold" saga. Similar plants are proposed in the District HQs on need and feasibility based approach.

The Shillong model has not been as efficient and productive. The synergy between the partners is not built on sound policy in management of the plant. There appears to be a lack of understanding on private and public role in the partnership. The garbage disposal issue handled casually for years, has finally erupted, together with the stench and stink of both the plant, management and the system or rather lack of one. The non-biodegradable items including plastics are being dumped since years together, on the slopes of the disposal site leading to severe air and water pollution. Lack of adequate returns to self sustain the venture must have influenced the private partner to discontinue regular operation of the plant. A well conceived project poorly executed. The Municipal Solid Waste Management and Handling Rules, 2000 clearly indicate that the State Govt. has to establish a sanitary landfill at the disposal site of the plant, where rejects-over 35% of the garbage, are dumped. On an average 1 hectare of land is required annually for dumping. Indiscriminate land filling at present site besides having adverse health impact on people living nearby shall be exposed to methane gas release which accounts for 50 to 60% of landfill gas accumulation. Umiam Lake below is also in danger of contamination from landfill lechaates. Hence, extension of landfill areas at the existing location shall be catastrophic unless latest technology to re-cycle plastic and

other non–bio degradable is installed to create
minimum rejects. The present status has evolved
due to years of unsanitary methods adopted for
disposal of solid waste in absence of sanitary
landfills. Diversion of land for solid waste disposal
would be impossible in near future considering
collection efficiency as 72.5%, depth 4 metres
of landfill site and waste density as 0.9 tonne/
cum (all average figures). ADB has taken up the
entire solid waste management sector for GSPA
based on approved CDP & vision document for
Shillong under JNNURM. The present plant
covers mostly municipal area of about 10 sq km
while settlements beyond municipal jurisdiction is
outside the purview of any scientific management
except for few Dorbars which manage the waste
locally with help of external agencies / NGOs,
while majority resort to burning.

Waste management is not merely dumping,
composting and landfill stacking. A successful
management chain has to initiate from individual
household level starting with source segregation
followed by minimum handling in primary/
secondary collection and transportation to
composting site. In our case the composting
plant was established without strengthening

the preliminary operations through awareness, education, capacity building and honing civic sense at the base level of the chain. A classic case of the adage "cart before the horse" syndrome. Therefore, holding present officials responsible for the mess accruing over the years is unfair. The right approach is to find a solution to this vexed issue through concerted efforts of all concerned. One of the most viable solution available to-day is the "waste to energy" treatment plants which has been found not only efficient but the end product could gap the increasing energy needs of concerned state.

As there are no policy guidelines to govern private public partnership, it is imperative to approach the issue with an open mind. This joint venture cannot be viewed in isolation, but more as a pilot project. A comprehensive appraisal of the partnership on a long term perspective is necessary to sustain the partnership. An uncompromising stance from any of the partners, may eventually lead to writing the obituary of this environment revitalization, civic amenity plant.

Another related vital issue which has the potential to affect the common man in a lethal form is lack of proper management of bio-medical waste. The

Bio-Medical Waste(Management & Handling Rules,1998(amended 2000) notified under Environment(Protection) Act 1986 is applicable to all who generate, handle and dispose. The rule provides for protection of human being and environment from this infectious and hazardous waste generated from health care (human and animals) and related facilities. It is mandatory for all such health care providers including pathological labs to set up requisite treatment facilities or transport to a common facility after segregation, packaging etc within 48 hours of generation. State Pollution Control Board is prescribed authority to implement the rules. A common BMW treatment facility has been commissioned only recently at Marten. It is important to monitor and review whether all generators(occupiers) have installed the treatment facility or joined the common facility as time provided for completing the same as per rules was till 31st December 2002. In case of non-compliance the defaulting occupiers are liable for several punitive action and punishment under section 15 of EP Act, 1986. Many occupiers are either without or set up negligible infrastructure to show a modicum of compliance. Important equipments are incinerator, autoclave, chemical treatment bath, needle & plastic shredder besides secured land fill etc. Very little information is available regarding implementation of different aspects of management, maintenance, submission and scrutiny of records and invoking of this law including punitive action initiated if any. A few hospitals and nursing homes from their location in crowded localities may end up creating more patients than they actually cure. Or is it another in genuine marketing strategy. It is high time for a comprehensive study and streamlining the entire system, in public interest, before another mayhem erupts.

13

Violation of law;
elusive penalty.

(Issue highlighted in the year 2012)

The present environment of standoff in the State has consciously or otherwise led to relegation of numerous important issues into the background or to a state of deadlock. Notable among them being the violation of Forest Act, 1980 by the cement plants in Jaintia Hills which has been established and duly accepted by MoEF as being true and directing the defaulters to seek clearance under FC Act, 1980. A number of articles, memorandum and PILs by NGOs and individuals resulted in the positive results. Although the concerned authorities, including State Forest & Environment Minister declared a few months back that penalty shall be imposed by the MoEF on all defaulting plants, nothing concrete has materialized till date. This dragging of feet may be "beneficial" to a select few but at what cost? Pollution of Lukha River water turning blue with poison discharge, being just one among the slew of environment degrading factors. Experience of the Lafarge Umiam Mining Pvt. Ltd case is a grim reminder that the inevitable can best be delayed but will catch up with baggage of retrospective liability. LUMPL in spite of being granted site, forest and environment clearance by the MoEF in 2001, had to seek fresh approval after it was established that mining of limestone was undertaken in forest areas by misrepresentation of facts, declaring mining in high forest areas as non-forest/barren land. All activities were stopped from 2007 till Supreme Court finally allowed functioning with prescribed penalties which the company promptly complied with in 2010. An attempt to circumvent the proven cases of violation in other cases and clear future hurdles, led to redefining of forest by hurriedly passing Meghalaya Forest Regulation (Amendment) Bill, 2012, by amending Meghalaya Forest Regulation (Application and Amendment) Act, 1973 in December last year. The sudden urgency to redefine forest without taking public opinion and maintaining optimal transparency is obviously not intended at enhancing conservation as it shall now take hundreds of hectares outside the purview of forest. Another important issue is (or was?) diversion of an additional area of around 1100 hectares of forest for mining of limestone

without inviting forest clearance provision under
FC Act, 1980. The purported snag in diversion
is that even the redefined version cannot take
care of the high percentage of forest cover in the
proposed areas!

According to informed sources, the apparent
reason for the "delay" in imposing the penalty
is attributed to formulation of the appropriate
norms for finalizing the quantum to be fixed
for each of the defaulting industries. If that
argument is true than the MoEF has only to
adhere in principle to its own guidelines issued,
based on Supreme Court ruling in fixing of
penalty in case of LUMPL which justifiably
be adopted as bench mark for all pending
cases. In addition to bearing the cost of raising
compensatory afforestation over double the area
violated and penal compensatory afforestation
over five times the area violated, the defaulting
industry shall have to shell out five times the
normal NPV with interest. The total area
under jurisdiction of the industries together
stand at around 2112 hectares. On a lenient
approximation even if 60% of the area is
categorized as forest, a staggering 1276 hectares
of forest area has been diverted compared to 100

hectares for which LUMPL has been penalized. Moreover, a sum of rupees ninety per tonne of limestone from the date of commencement of mining by violation of FC, Act has to be borne by the user agency. The entire amount as above has to be deposited with an SPV to be set up under the chairmanship of a Chief Secretary level official with provision for public representation, specifically for undertaking projects aimed at holistic and sustained development of the mining area and its vicinity extending up to a fixed radius. In relation to East Jaintia Hills, the total penalty amount accrued from all defaulting plants shall be to the tune of over a thousand crores. The funds if utilized judiciously can cover the entire district which shall witness a giant leap in all round development encompassing all sectors with potential to emerge as one of the most developed district of the country. And rehabilitation of worked over coal and limestone mines, which is on top of our environment friendly Chief Minister's agenda can also be achieved. There will be no compulsion to depend on alms in the form of CSR intervention or on government funds. While the actual mining areas will have to be demarcated and fenced to stop

"spill over" syndrome the State Government
will have to examine the circumstances under
which all such forest land was declared as non-
forest land besides setting up of an independent
Environment Department as in other states
to deal with all issues other than those under
purview of forest management.

14

Redefining forest to ensure unimpeded deforestation?

(Issue highlighted in the year 2013)

Meghalaya will now have a new definition of forest. A bizarre retrogressive step, which confirms with clarity, an approach of "re-defining after destruction". A covert move to redefine forest was in motion since last several years. It is not difficult to comprehend the motive behind such a move. In an era where conservation of forest is the priority, the amendment clearly seeks to obliterate whatever little forest cover exists in the State to facilitate and provide easy access and license to deforest with impunity, through diversion of high forest into non-forest status. This amendment comes after a saga of systematic destruction of virgin mature forest, mainly for establishing limestone mining in different locations of Jaintia Hills in Meghalaya. Heat generated by such gross violation, mostly by misleading the project proponents, appears to have given the motivation to seek cover by desperately making efforts to redefine forest. The move is to justify the diversion of forest land for non-forestry purpose through NOC granted earlier, projecting all such mature forest as "non-forest" or "private forest" and evade the applicability of FC Act 1980. Interestingly, United Khasi-Jaintia Hills Autonomous District (Management & Conservation of forests) Act, 1958 clearly defines forest as – "… an area where not less than 25 trees per acre or around 65 trees per hectare, reserved or unreserved or any other forest produce growing on such area which have been or are capable of being exploited for purpose of business or trade …. as "forest". This characterization is considered among the best in the country and comes closest to the Apex Court's definition after the ban on felling and one which is nearest to the ground reality. The recent amendment has deviated drastically. According to Meghalaya Forest (Amendment) Bill 2012, an area would be considered a forest if it is a compact or continuous tract of minimum four hectares of land, irrespective of ownership, where more than 250 naturally growing trees or more than 100 naturally growing bamboo clumps per hectare are present. Fixing of 4 hectares area as base level of calculation is a clever ploy to exploit the 5 hectare limitation, beyond which central clearance is mandatory under FC Act, 1980. **There are very few forest areas**

in Meghalaya to-day with such density of growing stock, particularly in a compact, contiguous block of 4 hectares. Hence, passing of the Act shall give legitimacy to freely destroy almost all available land of forest cover and divert to non forest activities. The intention is clearly to obtain "absolute freedom" over forest areas once such areas come out of the purview of the FC Act, 1980. With handful of land sharks, acquiring both agricultural and forest land all over the State at break neck speed, time is not far when the majority of indigenous population will lose even their small individual and clan land holdings and be reduced to landless entities in their own homeland.

In the historic T. N Godavarman Thirumulpad Vs Union of India (W.P 202 of 1995), wherein it has been clarified that the word 'forest' must be understood according to the dictionary meaning of the term, irrespective of the nature of ownership and classification thereof. There was no confusion regarding the definition in the United Khasi-Jaintia Hills Autonomous District (Management & Conservation of forests) Act, 1958 for last forty five years and the same was made more clear and simple by legalizing the dictionary meaning. As a result, large areas under good forest cover which were outside the purview of the Forest (Conservation) Act, 1980 came under the Act. Whereas the present amendment, in contravention to the Supreme Court ruling, takes out large tracts of forest area outside the purview of forest for easy access. This is against the spirit and principle of the Apex Court's order. It now becomes easier for project proponents to avoid FC, Act 1980, by clearing the land of vegetation first and then apply for NOC, once the stipulation of the amendment is achieved. Moreover, in 1998 the Supreme Court in context of the same PIL directed that working plans for all forest divisions shall be prepared by the state governments and would have to be approved by the central government. It was clarified that the term 'State Government' would also include District Councils constituted under Schedule VI of the Constitution of India. Thus, in absence of working plans which contains extensive details of a particular forest, including mode of operation et al, all land, water bodies etc under control of the three district councils and Forest & Environment Department are forest, pending categorization and approval of working plans. Consequently, NOC etc in matters of forest to make the amendment operative has to be based on approved working plan.

Moreover, the claim that the amended Act shall not have "retrospective affect" is hard to digest. As a desperate measure to come out from the "NOC quicksand" the High Level Committee constituted by the State Government to enquire into the FC, Act 1980 violations in Jaintia Hill mining areas, was dissolved in great urgency, when it was about to submit its findings. The dissolution was resorted to by interpreting a Supreme Court judgement in IA no 1868 of 6th July 2011, on a retrospective perception although it was more of a suggestion or advisory for the future, open to understanding since it speaks of *project proponents claim* on status of land being non-forest and desirability.

Another question is why the urgency now?. This urgency and redefining should have been undertaken prior to issuing indiscriminate NOC in high forest declaring them as non forest or "deemed" forest.

In case, re-definition of forest is imperative and genuine grounds exist for review of "dictionary meaning", an extensive silvicultural survey, based on sample plots, all over the state, has to be undertaken to obtain real time data and information including situation status at ground level. Such exercise for review has to be based on major "forest type" of our state, mainly the two principal categories ie tropical and deciduous, commensurate to the canopy density of each type, irrespective of geographical and political boundaries. Arbitrary definition without scientific study, simply by increasing the number of trees per hectare is definitely not in the interest of at least sustaining the existing forest cover of the state.

It will be interesting to wait and watch if the present amendment is used as a shield for sins of the past or is a weapon to be used to engage in wanton violations under protection and cover of the amended Act. Both shall be catastrophic for the future of forest cover and general state of environment including the biodiversity status which has already been relegated to abysmal depth.

15

Dangers of exploiting ground water.

(Issue highlighted in the year 2006)

The ground shattering loud noise of truck mounted water drills are a common sight all over the country. On enquiry it is learnt that a number of such water drill infrastructure are stationed at Shillong since over a decade with couple of months advance booking necessary to engage one. This is a clear evidence of the extent to which ground water is being harnessed within Greater Shillong areas. It is not always need based but an "additional security" of ensuring excess, far beyond ones requirement. This is a very dangerous trend for the future. India is among the countries that will be worst hit by water scarcity with an estimated 100 million people facing drought conditions, reflecting ominous portent of a dry and barren future. Meghalaya together with other north eastern states of the country, particularly the hills are perilously poised. It will not take long compared to the plains, for the situation to take an abrupt turn for the worst. It is not a question of non-availability of water but total ignorance and lack of initiative to conserve water, resulting in bulk of the rain water flowing down the hilly terrain into the plains. The severe water crisis at Sohra especially during dry months, in spite of being one of the highest rainfall locales in the world, is definitely a forewarning of the approaching danger. Ground water exploitation particularly energized mechanical in nature with capacity of output ranging from 2500 ltrs per hour and above need to be regulated strictly, if not totally banned, except for community supply schemes in selected rural areas where no other feasible source of supply is viable.

A major segment of the population is provided with surface water, emanating mostly from springs, streams and rivulets originating or flowing through the catchments. However, with ecological degradation of majority catchments in and around Shillong, the output from this primary source has been rapidly declining. The major source of piped water supply is GSWSS which is augmenting its generation and distribution to cover more areas under a scheme approved under JNNURM. The surface water generated and distributed through the network of Civic bodies is improving to meet the demand of Shillong and its suburbs although the situation deteriorates to a stage of water scarcity in many areas of the capital during dry months. In order to overcome such stress conditions, an increasing number of residents are taking recourse to harnessing of ground water by establishing bore or deep tube wells. This development which was more evident in areas located outside municipal jurisdiction due to absence of government supply, is gaining momentum with municipal jurisdiction. Groundwater, as a natural resource can augment supply during the water scarcity periods. In order to maintain this potential, a hydraulic equilibrium must be established between availability and utilization. Groundwater exploitation increasingly became inevitable in certain localities due to scarcity of regular supply of piped surface water. However, with present easing of the situation, measures must be initiated at this stage to ensure that no over exploitation of this source is allowed. Wells were unheard of in Shillong even in the eighties. Such wells basically cater to the need of an individual settlement, harnessing far in excess to actual water requirement. The result is over exploitation of ground water without any initiative for augmenting natural infiltration of rainwater or surface run off into the underground formation. The proliferation of energized wells has to be restricted, since such wells have depleted ground water all over the country ranging from 1 to 3 meters a year depending on their location. In hilly terrain, the decline shall be much higher. Such wells can be allowed, if matching replenishment measures are ensured. Over extraction of ground water, lead to intrusion of polluted water into aquifers, resulting in problems of excess iron besides arsenic and fluoride. Ground water is facing an equally serious threat from contamination by various effluents together with fertilizers and pesticides from farm run-offs. Recycle of effluents, domestic sullage and sewage not only conserve vast volumes of water, but also protects the environment by reducing pollution.

The best way to replenish a bore well is through rain water. Infiltration of rainwater or surface run off into the underground formation is facilitated by different artificial methods like water spreading; recharge pits, trenches, shafts or direct diversion to existing wells. The choice and effectiveness of a particular method is governed by local hydro-geological formation, soil status and end use. Rooftop rainwater harvesting system is most feasible and appropriate from the point of availability, technical suitability and economic viability. Moreover, instead of the common approach of canalizing rooftop run-off to drains, the outlets must be connected to existing wells to serve as recharge points. All such steps should be aimed at maintaining the water table at a pre-determined constant level to which extraction has to be limited. This can be achieved through a law which shall provide for monitoring of all existing energized wells, including approval for establishing new ones, subject to suitable arrangement(s) made in the ground, well in advance for recharge. A check and balance approach is essential if we want to ensure an optimum water table and also avoid serious health hazards arising due to arsenic or fluoride contamination of ground water. A strategy to implement ground water recharge needs to be launched with concerted efforts of Government, Civic Bodies and stakeholders. In fact few Durbar Shnongs(local tribal traditional body for grass root governance) had initiated strict regulation on bore wells during 2005-06. The recently modified building bye-laws of Meghalaya Urban Development Authority have rightly made rain water harvesting mandatory for all new construction. It needs to be taken a step ahead for existing buildings to follow suit with specific technical guidelines on how to execute the concept. And above all a realistic appraisal of ground water potential of Greater Shillong Urban Agglomerate has to be undertaken with assistance of Central Ground Water Commission, followed by "water zoning" to identify areas where and to what extent harness of ground water is feasible and areas where the same is not recommended. On completion of the exercise, a procedure must be adopted for regulation by concerned agency of granting permission by clearly specifying bore size, discharge rate, output etc allowed to an applicant based on finding of zoning.

16

Conserve water in nature's bucket!

(Issue highlighted in the year 2006)

The biggest impact of climate change on humans and the environment will occur through water. Water availability has an innate variability in occurrence and managing this inconsistency is actually water management. Climate change threatens to make this variability much more acute and complex, resulting in more uncertainty in the quantity and quality of water supply over the long term. Climate change is altering the timing, magnitude and duration of precipitation. In addition, human-induced climate change poses a new set of challenges, since the management system can no longer plan, design and operate hydrologic systems based on past statistics. This new risk has to be taken into account in policy planning and operations at all levels – national and local. Water resource management will have to be done for a hydrological unit such as drainage basin or a hill top catchment as a whole, taking into account surface and ground water for sustainable use. All individual developmental projects and proposals should be formulated and considered within the framework of such an overall plan with an integrated and environmentally sound approach, keeping in the view the socio-economic aspects and need.

The hills of north east India, particularly state capitals like Shillong, Aizawl, Kohima & Itanagar are in the threshold of facing a water stress situation. According to international standards, a region is defined as water stressed and water scarce if annual per capita water availability falls below 1,700 and 1000 cubic metres respectively. The salty oceans and seas hold 97% of world's water and out of the balance only 0.007 % is drinkable. As per World Resource Institute, India is one of the ten water rich nations of the world. Yet we have millions of hectares of dry arid land, famine, and suicides due to water stress conditions. This phenomenon itself speaks volume on our management system or lack of it. The per capita annual freshwater capacity in the country is likely to go below 1200 cubic metres by 2025. These figures are basically standards derived on majority plain lands and accordingly the bench mark for hills has to be considered at a lower value. It establishes with clarity that the situation will be far worse and arrive much earlier in the hills. This is primarily due to the fact that bulk of rainfall in the hills flow down to the plains, except the volume retained by catchments- natures own "buckets".

The North-eastern hill ranges covering all NE States extend over Bangladesh and northern Myanmar, touching the southern slopes of the Brahmaputra valley and the northern, eastern and southern slopes of the Barak valley. The Meghalaya plateau covers the entire state of Meghalaya and the Karbi Anglong hills of Assam. The climate and rainfall of the area varies considerably across the region. Encircled by hills and plateaus, rainfall varies even more than temperatures. The average annual rainfall reaches a peak of 13,390 mm in the Cherrapunji-Mawsynram region of Meghalaya. But areas that fall in the rain shadow region of the Meghalaya plateau need irrigation. While the northern slopes of the Brahmaputra valley receive an annual average rainfall of 2,500 mm, the area south of the valley and the northern part of Meghalaya receive an annual rainfall of about 2,000 mm. This clearly reflects that water resources potential of the region is the largest in the entire country. Given its heavy rainfall, it also has abundant groundwater resources. But only a small part of the region has been studied to estimate the groundwater potential. The maximum scope for development of groundwater exists in Assam, Tripura and Arunachal Pradesh. The available surface water resources have hardly been tapped because of the rugged nature of the terrain. Hence, cultivation in the region is largely rain fed and shifting in nature. Yet, water conservation by the indigenous population has received priority for centuries. There are documented instances of some indigenous rainwater harvesting systems used for cultivation, of which some are ingenious. Settled agriculture is practised in the form of irrigated terrace cultivation in parts of Nagaland and a few villages of Meghalaya. Channels are dug to irrigate these fields. The other notable indigenous source of irrigation is the bamboo irrigation system found in parts of Meghalaya, Mizoram and Nagaland. Further, no organized water management regime has ever been followed in most of the states except in Mizoram to some extent.

Recent studies have revealed that large Himalayan glaciers are retreating at a rate of more than 30 metres a year, resulting in over 20% reduction in glacier area since the 1980s. This together with reduction in solid precipitation in hilly regions will directly affect water resources for domestic supply, irrigated agriculture, hydropower generation and other water-dependent activities.

India's National Water Policy emphasizes continued government control over water resources, ignoring pleas by environmental groups to involve local communities in order to overcome threatening shortages. The National Water Policy will remain inert and ineffectual because it is far removed from the two simple but important challenges of water management today -- rainwater harvesting and small community initiatives. India has been hit by water shortages because of a shift away from traditional methods of storing and using rainwater to exploiting rivers, by damming them up through costly and centralized irrigation, power and drinking water schemes. Apart from big hydro power dams and irrigation systems, the government has encouraged the digging of millions of tube wells and bore wells energized by electric and diesel-driven pumps that now provide half of the country's irrigation. Rural areas can also be heavily dependent on groundwater where

50% of irrigation water and 80% of drinking water, much of which is brought to the surface by a network of over 5 million hand-pumped wells. As more and more water is pumped out of the ground, there has been a dramatic lowering of the water table across the country. Rajendra Singh, who in 2001 won the Ramon Magsaysay award for his efforts in turning the village of Arvari in western Rajasthan state's arid Alwar district into a lush, green area, had to face bureaucratic wrath that deemed his efforts illegal. His efforts had been successful partly because he turned to building small earthen check dams to impound rainwater. Considering the growing awareness about climate change and the India's National Water Policy emphasis on continued government control over water resources, ignoring pleas by environmental groups to involve local communities in order to overcome looming shortages is proving disastrous. Water Policy should be people-centred and recognize communities as the rightful custodians of water. The need to ease exclusive control by the government machinery over water resources is imperative to ensure a paradigm shift to participatory, essentially local management of water resources.

Management of the water resources for diverse uses should be done by adopting a participatory approach; involving not only the various governmental agencies but also the users and other stakeholders in an effective and decisive way in various aspects of planning, design, development and management of the water resources schemes. Necessary legal and institutional changes are necessary at various levels for the purpose duly ensuring appropriate role for women. Water Users' Associations and the local bodies such as Municipalities/Dorbars/NGOs should particularly be involved in the operation, maintenance and management of water infrastructures / facilities at appropriate levels progressively with a view to eventually transfer the management of such facilities to the user groups / local bodies. In a rural context, groundwater provides the mainstay for agricultural irrigation and will be the key to providing additional resources for food security. However, concerns are growing over the sustainability of individual water sources, and there is a growing need for management strategies that recognize the complex linkages that exist between groundwater supplies, urban land use and effluent supervision.

Most water stressed and scarce countries have adopted the concept of Virtual water. This is essentially water that is embedded in food or other products needed for its production. Trade in virtual water allows water scarce countries to import high water consuming products while exporting low water consuming products and in this way making water available for more emergent purposes like human consumption. Further, "water footprint" similar to carbon is also in vogue. The water footprint of a nation is related to dietary habits of people. High consumption of meat or food originating from irrigated land, to cite an example, brings along a large water footprint. Finally, nations in warm climate zones have relatively high water consumption for their domestic food production resulting in a larger water footprint.

At an individual level, it is useful to show the footprint as a function of food diet and consumption patterns. It is time for us in the hills to adopt more pragmatic and innovative ideas to reduce our water footprints and conserve ground water including recharge of aquifers to avoid a water calamity.

Thus the immediate priority will be to draw an Action Plan for Water sanctuaries and creating associated infrastructure for providing water security for sustainable development. It is high time for the Government machinery, civil society, NGOs etc to initiate tangible measures on the ground through projects and programmes conceived, formulated, implemented, monitored and evaluated in close consultation with the stake holding communities following the approach of 'Peoples Participation and Appraisal'. The transition from water stress to water scarce condition will not take long if the present ground shattering rhetoric in seminars, lectures and workshops continue without action on the ground and creating public awareness of the impending danger.

17

Harvest rain water to check wet desert syndrome.

(Issue highlighted in the year 2008)

The ecological degradation of Sohra or commonly known all over the world as Cherrapunjee – the wettest place on earth is ironically also termed as a "wet desert". What a dichotomy! Sohra receives around 2000 mm of average annual rainfall and yet undergoes severe water stress condition for over six months in a year. This clearly confirms the grim reality that neither allocation of fund nor availability of water shall be of any tangible benefit without sound planning and judicious utilization.

The emerging water stress condition is a consequence of unplanned use and misuse of natural resources coupled with total ignorance and lack of initiative to conserve water. This has resulted in bulk of the rain water flowing down the hilly terrain into the plains. There is hardly any effort to conserve this valuable component, required on a sustained basis in perpetuity to sustain life. The time is ripe to revert back to nature and be guided by its numerous inherent mechanisms. Nature has its own ingenious way of purifying and recycling water and maintaining equilibrium.

The situation in the hills of NE India shall face similar situation if corrective measures are not initiated immediately. The lack of water recycling and careful management will invariably lead to water stress conditions. Accordingly, all the water allowed to flow down is forever lost. It is thus imperative to conserve and retain maximum possible water before it goes down. The mining areas of the State particularly are exposed to the additional hazard of contamination of water and destruction of aquifers – store house of ground water; due to unscientific and rampant mining operations. A concrete and viable method is harvesting of rain water which is the first form and principal source of water in the hydrological cycle. The ecology movement since 1960's onwards has postulated the theory that people must cultivate the habit to live, within the limitations of earth's infinite supply of resources. Mizoram has embraced this philosophy in letter and spirit. As the situation here is more complex than other states due to less rainfall, harvesting of rainwater has become the convention to tide over the lean season. A water saving consciousness is palpable at Aizawl, reflecting an exercise beyond mere conservation or management.

Water harvesting is primarily direct collection and storage of rain water together with allied activities aimed at prevention of losses through evaporation and seepage. The stored water can either be used directly or recharged into the ground water. The concept which is a fundamental approach to ease water shortage, also allows individual / household control over generation and distribution. It is essential to adopt this strategy as more than 90% of precipitation takes place during monsoon, out of which 75 – 80% is lost and thus unavailable for utilization. The common agenda should be to collect as much rain water as possible to narrow the gap between supply and demand, particularly as reserve or buffer during prolonged dry spell.

A major segment of the State's population is provided with surface water, emanating mostly from springs, streams and rivulets originating or flowing through the catchments.

However, with ecological degradation of majority catchments due to various adverse factors impinging directly on denigration of catchments, the output from this primary source is rapidly declining. Thus, surface water generated and distributed is grossly inadequate to meet the demand. The situation deteriorates to an acute stage of water crisis in many areas of the north east during dry months.

Some amount of rainwater which falls on earth's surface percolates through the soil and are stored in the interstices of the soil or rock that forms the earth. It is similar to water being stored in a sponge. Groundwater aquifers are formed as a consequence of infiltration spread over years of successive rains on merging with existing groundwater. Streams, lakes and groundwater are all secondary sources of water. At present we are mostly dependant on such secondary sources together with ground water. It is forgotten that rain is the ultimate source that feeds all these sources and thus remain ignorant regarding the prime importance of rainwater.

The basic principle of rain water harvesting is to make optimum use of rainwater at the place where it falls. Conservation of rainwater is

mandatory failing which the quantum and degree
of rainfall becomes irrelevant, until tapped to
recharge ground aquifers or stored for direct use.
Rainwater harvesting is deliberate collection
of rainwater within a "catchment" and storage
in manmade structures or natural depressions.
Catchment includes rooftops, compounds, rocky
surfaces, hill slopes, artificially prepared semi or
impervious land surface. Harvesting begins and
ends with the rainy season and users are left with
a fixed volume of water until the following rainy
monsoon. Artificial recharge is the processes of
augmenting natural infiltration of rainwater or
surface run off into the underground formation by
different artificial methods like water spreading,
recharge pits, trenches, bore wells, shafts or
direct diversion to existing wells. The choice and
effectiveness of a particular method is governed
by local hydro-geological formation, soil status
and end use. The total amount of water received
due to rainfall over a fixed area is termed as the
rainwater endowment of that area and the volume
that can be actually harvested is called the water
harvesting potential which is equal to rainfall
(mm) x collection efficiency. The rainwater
collection efficiency is estimated after taking
into consideration loss accruing on account of

evaporation, spillage, run-off coefficient and first flush wastage. Rooftop rainwater harvesting system is most feasible and appropriate from the point of availability, technical suitability and economic viability. Instead of the common approach of canalizing rooftop run-off to drains, the outlets are connected through a pipe into gravel filled trenches, pits or existing wells to serve as recharge points. Rainwater collected from rooftops is soft, free from mineral pollutants and contrary to popular beliefs water quality improves over time, during storage as impurities settle in the tank and most pathogens gradually die out.

Rain water harvesting and water re-cycling has to be made a compulsory component in building codes while granting permission for construction of buildings. Moreover, it must be made mandatory for existing Government buildings, private and public institutions, housing society's et al to establish water harvesting facilities within a fixed time frame. Moreover, emphasis on harnessing and conservation including harvesting of rainwater is imperative, instead of solely concentrating on creating storage infrastructure and laying pipelines which otherwise may end up storing and transmitting air in due course.

18

Resurgence of traditional medicines.

(Issue highlighted in the year 2004)

India in ancient times was most modern in its science and technology. The Ayurvedic heritage which deals with the use of medicinal plants traces its roots, over five thousand years ago, to the Himalayan region. According to legend, a conference was held in this province where the greatest sages of India met to discuss their knowledge on the art of healing and exchange "notes". The term Ayurveda (Sanskrit words, "ayus"- life and "veda"- knowledge) is believed to have emerged from this "conclave". The genesis and veracity of the story notwithstanding, our country is endowed with natural conditions which enable the growth of virtually every type of medicinal or aromatic plant. India is rich in all the three levels of bio-diversity- species, genetic and habitat. The vibrant genetic resource base has emerged from over 426 biomes, representing different habitat, each considered one of the richest in the world.

The North East with the altitudinal variation in vegetation ranging from the temperate to alpine is a major repository of plant diversity in the world. This region is one of the 18-bio diversity hot spots of the world, accounting for more almost 60% of total plant species available in India and contributes significantly to the recognition of India as one of the world's top mega diversity nations. Consequently, there has been a rich and vibrant heritage of knowledge in traditional medicine among the indigenous population, similar to Ayurveda, Unani and Sidha system that has been practiced for centuries in rural India. On a rough estimate, around 200 species of plants including herbs, shrubs and trees are used for preventive and curative besides self-treatment applications in this region. W.H.O. estimated that 80% of the population of developing countries relies on the traditional medicines. The region is a veritable treasure trove of a variety of natural resources, available in abundance. This has motivated the traditional healers for centuries to utilize a small segment of this rich resource, to develop their individual concoction, for treatment of different ailments. The traditional system of cure has evolved with passage of time, conforming to intrinsic knowledge of medicinal plants among the local "herbal practitioners". Over exploitation of forest and fossil fuels has not only resulted in colossal depletion of such reserves but also set in motion the process of environmental degradation. Now with the rising demand and global interest in medicinal plants and traditional system of health care, this particular resource base has become the cynosure of both national and international pharmaceutical industries and research institutes.

The North East together with other Himalayan states, though bestowed with nature's rich bounty is economically under developed. This stark reality makes the indigenous people of the entire belt vulnerable to external manoeuvrings, aimed at economic abuse of the rich resource base. It is necessary to be vigilant, as collection of medicinal and herbal plants from the wild is gaining momentum. In fact, this exercise has been in process for quite some time. However, due to lack of awareness and abundance of most species in the villages and rural segment of all these states, coupled with inhospitable terrain, collection of these plants has been continuing in a clandestine manner. A dramatic increase in export with over 90% of the demand assembled from the wild, has led to hundreds of species being threatened with extinction due to over harvesting, destructive collection methods and conversion of habitats to crop based agriculture. A typical case is related to the small coniferous Himalayan yew (*Taxus bacata*), rendered virtually endangered. Taxol – the most successful anti cancer drug, derived from this species was developed subsequently, by utilizing a sizeable bio resource exported from this region for R&D together with Pacific yew (Taxus brevifolia). The patent right is now the sole property of an American firm- Bristol Myaers. There are innumerable cases of cross- border smuggling of valuable bio- resource collected from the forests of this region. There is no affective mechanism to regulate and monitor large-scale collection in high forests. As the collection areas fall within the jurisdiction of forest, the concerned department or respective district councils are responsible for protection. However, due to various constraints, it is not possible to even prevent illegal felling of tress or poaching of wild life like rhino. It is thus beyond comprehension, how the medicinal plants including herbs and shrubs, spread over hundreds of kilometres can be protected and their unauthorized collection brought to a halt.

A broad based intensive investigation of all available medicinal plants of the region, followed by inventorization and documentation has to be accorded top priority. This vital exercise, on completion, will provide an insight into the actual growing stock of potentially valuable species. The extraordinary progress in bio-technology has stimulated the search for compounds from biological origin, which could be promising drugs in the future.

The policy makers in GOI, some State government(s), including a few committed Institutions, have realized the immense potential in cultivation of medicinal plants. It has been accorded due importance and placed in the same strata with other priority sectors like Tourism, Horticulture and I.T. for development of the region. This is a step in the right direction, as farming is in harmony with traditional tribal culture and hence will find wide acceptability. It has the potential to emerge as a viable income generating alternative together with bamboo. The marginal farmers and small growers at the grass root level including those who have been affected by the ban on timber will benefit directly, ensuring emancipation of rural economy. This decision is most heartening. What is disturbing however is the unorganized manner in which some projects are being taken up without proper reconnaissance of ecological requirements, absence of field trials to ascertain the limiting factors and determine the commercial viability of different species selected for a particular location. As substantial funds are available from different sources including grants and incentives, a number of projects has been envisaged without proper planning and detailed study of site factors, adaptability of species etc. This perilous trend will prove counter productive and in all likelihood become another contentious subsidy and incentive driven venture, to benefit a select few.

Cultivation of medicinal plants is not a business enterprise like manufacturing. It is something much more intricate, requiring intensive management techniques starting from the nursery stage to planting, establishment of planting materials and implementation of subsequent maintenance regime, with diligence. There is no short route to success or instant result, as there is a very thin line between success and failure. All medicinal plant species will not grow at each and every locality. The determining factors are altitude, climate- macro & micro, soil profile etc to name a few. It is therefore imperative, to set up trial plots to study the growth and yield performance of each species, based on field study and practical enumeration before embarking on large scale cultivation of a particular species. Moreover, due to growing demand for herbal drugs and cosmetics, the biodiversity rich north east is already facing pressure on natural populations of medicinal and aromatic flora. Conservation of this plant diversity, mainly potentially useful species, can be achieved by adopting effective strategy to protect and nurture the plants in their native ecosystems (in situ). Alternately, the genetic diversity can be conserved away from its natural habitat (ex situ). The two approaches, can act as complementary to back up each other while promoting commercial cultivation of medicinal & aromatic plants on a sustainable basis. As majority of medicinal plants are collected from the wild, the resource base are gradually shrinking. It is thus imperative to undertake cultivation of important species, mainly those which are in demand commercially, simultaneously with plants that are facing extinction.

Medicinal plants market in the country is unorganized. Such plants, being living resource are exhaustible if overused and sustainable if used with care and wisdom. Global market data reflect an expanding opportunity in the herbal sector. Annual market growth rate of 15% in India compared to 7% globally provides immense scope in this sector. It is necessary to take up a systematic approach towards cultivation of medicinal and herbal plant produce of international quality. In order to attain this standard, high safety and quality regimes must be maintained together with healthy manufacturing practices. According to World Health Organization, the current market of herbal drugs, which is more than double of modern synthetic drugs, stands at 70 billion US $ and projected to reach 5 trillion US $ by 2050. India in spite of such rich legacy and tradition, accounts for roughly 500 million US $ and is placed much lower than China with 50 billion US $ and even Thailand with 2.5 US $.

The National Medicinal Plant Board under the Ministry of Health & Family Welfare, GOI, set up for development of medicinal & aromatic plants, has taken a number of initiatives to accelerate the pace of growth in this sector. A major achievement has been to shortlist around 40 species of medicinal and aromatic plants suitable for commercial cultivation together with credit facilities from financial institutions at low interest rates, available to interested farmers. This sector has the potential to generate direct and indirect employment to minimum 10 lakh people. A holistic planning perspective can ensure this sector becoming the biggest mass based economic activity in the north east.

19

Unsung nature conservationists.

Conservation of forest and environment is neither the exclusive domains of environment activist like the Bahugunas, Patkars, Mehtas etc nor the host of NGOs advocating the cause throughout our country. The concept in fact had been firmly entrenched in the tribal psyche since centuries, particularly in the north east, when few in the country realized the importance of safeguarding the environment for posterity. The life of a tribal, till the last couple of decades, had been intricately linked to the forest. There has been a healthy and strong symbiotic relationship between the two. The existence of a tribal, particularly in villages, was in total and complete harmony with the forest, which was his natural abode. This unique relationship gave rise to crusaders of conservation all over northeast who motivated their brethren accordingly. The anxiety for protecting their habitat was inherent and spontaneous. Consequently, their involvement was absolute, associated with innovative strategy executed in all sincerity and dedication. As all such efforts were low profile, undertaken in an era when media publicity was virtually unknown, there was none to sing paeans of their contribution and commitment in upholding the cause of nature. Conservation of adequate reserve whether natural, material or otherwise is normally not an issue for human apprehension or priority particularly when it involves an entire tribe, community or race. Such social concerns usually emerge from individuals with foresight and practical wisdom. The need for preserving something that is already scarce or facing extinction is a delayed reaction, when immediate curative measures prevail over all other considerations. Under such circumstances too, there are few who venture to take the initiative with sincerity of purpose. The situation changed drastically during the last two decades, when "commercial marauders" from the mainland successfully convinced a sizeable section of tribals that "money actually grows on trees" and are meant to be sacrificed to meet the requirements of modern amenities. The enticement to sell the treasures bestowed by nature and inherited from their ancestors for a song was overwhelming. The rationalists' voice of reasoning emanating from both the region and the mainland were subdued in the chorus for instant and easy returns. The outflow of wealth and natural resources from the region was possibly a process linked to the course of joining the mainstream

A classic saga of conservation is reflected in the deed of erstwhile tribal Chiefs, commonly known as "Angs", of the Noctes- a vibrant and one of the two major tribes, inhabiting Tirap district of Arunachal Pradesh. The "Angs" of the two group of villages namely Namsang and Borduria exhibiting total clarity of vision way back in 1948, entered into separate agreements with His Excellency the Governor of Assam on 3rd November, 1948 and 5th September, 1948 respectively by which both the Chiefs leased out their forest areas measuring 107.62 Sq.Km and 38.10Sq.Km. respectively, for a period of 50 years to the Government. The lease has been renewed again with modifications after expiry. The forests thus leased out to the Government were notified into reserved forests in October 1962, primarily for ensuring scientific management by the Forest Department. The predominant tropical wet evergreen forest growing naturally in the area is one of the richest in the world in terms of value and bio diversity. As per agreement, the net revenue earned from the forests are to be shared between the 'Angs' (Chiefs) and the Government in the ratio of 75:25. There is also the provision for payment of certain fixed amount annually to the Chief of Namsang and Borduria to meet their personal needs. The "Angs" probably had a premonition of things to come, mainly the approaching pressure on the rich forest resource besides apprehending likely snags in the way of utilizing their share of revenue in worthwhile projects and schemes. They realized the importance of preserving the rich forest wealth with the idea to derive tangible benefits on a sustained basis in perpetuity for the people, from the increment in growth attained by the forest annually. The basic concept was to harvest the increment or "interest" and conserve the original forest or "principal".

With this end in view, the "Angs" entered into another agreement in 1960 with the Political Officer (now D.C.) and Director of Forests (now P.C.C.F.), N.E.F.A. administration for formation of a Trust, with both the officials designated as Trustees besides the two "Angs". The Trustees are authorized to receive the lease rent of the forest and utilize it for the social, educational and economic upliftment and common welfare of the people of Namsang-Borduria group of villages in particular and of Tirap District in general. The Trust thus created with the resources from Namsdang-Borduria reserve forests is termed as 'NAMSANG BORDURIA TRUST FUND' or N.B.F. The detailed procedures were drawn-up for executing and operating this particular Trust (fund) wherein the Deputy Commissioner Tirap Dist., Khonsa was authorized to administer the fund with the advice and guidance of NBF Advisory Committee comprising of ten members drawn from social workers, prominent public leaders of the area and other Departmental Heads of the District. In order to augment the income of the Trust for wider activities, investments are also made with profitable agencies to ensure sustained returns.

The main areas for development identified and sponsored by the fund are:-

a) Land development for permanent cultivation.

b) Development of road communication among Namsang-Borduria group of villages.

c) Improvement of water supply and sanitation.

d) Construction of Schools, Hospitals, Namghars etc.

e) Soil conservation measures, including creation and maintenance of village forests and nurseries.

f) Grants-in-Aid:

   i) for relief from hardship in case of natural calamities like flood, fire, earthquake etc.

   ii) for procurement of power tillers and tractors, farm machinery, seeds and fertilisers etc.

   iii) for setting up small business enterprise, agricultural or live stock farms etc.

g) Loans on easy terms of repayment to the beneficiaries of the fund for improvement of their housing and economic growth.

h) Allowances and Honoraria:

   i) Monthly allowances/honoraria to Chiefs and Leaders of the area for supervision of the development and welfare activities implemented by N.B.F.

ii) Stipends to the deserving students belonging to the Namsang-Borduria group of villages.

Further, pursuing the spirit of the Trust Deed, in order to organise educational activities, two sub-trusts have been created through two separate Deeds of Agreement respectively with the Secretary, Ramkrishna Mission, Belurmath, in 1971 and Secretary, Ramkrishna Sarada Mission, Dakshineswar, in 1972. As a result, two reputed Higher Secondary Schools, one for boys at Narottam Nagar and another for girls at Khonsa came into existence. These two esteemed institutions financed by NBF are imparting quality education to the people of Tirap District in particular and that of Arunachal Pradesh in general.

A number of development activities are undertaken in different spheres from this Trust Fund. Annual Grants are paid to the College, University and technical students belonging to Tirap District. At present over 100 students are on roll of annual grants. Special financial assistance is also awarded to the needy and deserving students of this district, in addition to providing aid for the deficit schools of the district as and when required. The trust fund is also utilized for granting relief to the people affected by natural calamities and as aid to the needy for specialized medical treatment outside the State. The Trust has also established a number of units for self-employment of women and unemployed youth.

The Trust has been playing a pivotal role for promoting and preserving the century old tradition and custom of the indigenous population of the district by establishing number of community halls like Rang Som Hum, Namghars, Village Morongs etc. and extending grants-in-aid for celebration of indigenous festivals and rituals.

A 80 bedded modern hospital and Nursing School, spread over an area of 175 acres has been established at Pullong located at a distance of 20 kms from Khonsa. The entire cost of around Rs 15 crores has been borne from internal resources of the Trust.

The imposition of ban on timber felling, conversion and trade by the Supreme Court has virtually dried up the only source of fund inflow to the Trust by almost Rs 5 crores annually.

Paucity of funds have adversely affected majority of development schemes. The Trust is presently functioning with the interest accrued not from the forest but the surplus from previous earnings received as lease rent from the Government of Arunachal Pradesh.

The prudence of the "Angs" in leasing out of their forests stand vindicated to a large extent. However, they could not have visualized the present situation although the state of affairs would have been much worse if preventive measures were not initiated by them immediately after independence. It is a matter for serious introspection whether the lessee has been able to live up to the expectation and spirit of the agreement as envisaged by the "Angs" of Namsang and Borduria.

The situation in Meghalaya had been better than many other locales of the country. We were blessed with a dream ecological system including rich bio diversity, well balanced and vibrant. To-day we are precariously poised in losing what nature had bestowed on us and the past generations had conserved with diligence. The traditional custom of the indigenous tribal community whose life was intricately linked to nature had laid down self regulatory stipulations aimed at 'consume with care – concern for others to follow". Regulation for focusing on the main things we consume and waste - water, food, energy and all natural resources like forests and animal products. The classification of forest, into "LawLyngdoh", "LawKyntang", "Law Niam"; are forests set apart on religious purpose and hitherto managed or controlled by the "Lyngdoh" - on whom the religious ceremonies for the particular locality or village is entrusted. The sacred groves in many areas of Khasi and Jaintia Hills of Meghalaya bear testimony to the innate commitment to forest conservation much before any forest act or rule came into existence. In addition there are other classes of forest like Law- a dong and Law- Shnong; which are village forests hitherto reserved by the villagers them-selves for conserving water, etc; for the use of the villagers. The concept of protecting the catchments which are nature's store houses of water is clearly evident in the traditional wisdom. This approach has also been primarily responsible for conserving the last vestige of catchment areas which has been the principal source of water supply for people of Shillong in Meghalaya for decades. The pristine forest was handed over by Raid Laban Durbar to the government for scientific management and control. The aquifers located in this forest feed the five major streams namely Umjesai, Wahjallynoh, Madan Laban, Patakhana, and Wahrisa which are all flow through the Raid Laban Forest area. Durbar Shnong is a democratic and traditional grass root institution of indigenous population for local self governance and administration at the locality or village level, free from direct government control.

Classification of forest was meant for a specific purpose, aimed at conservation, to serve the community for generations to come. These are few of the multiple initiatives which have been violated at will to serve interests of a few. The older generations may not have dreamt big but had a clear vision and premonition of how things may evolve with time and increasing population. The practical approach was to ensure enough for ones need and not for the present day unbridled greed, which has prompted such wanton destruction and over exploitation of every sphere of the environment.

20

Harnessing renewable energy.
(Issue highlighted in the year 2004)

The extensive extraction of fossil fuels has led to total denigration of global environment, both in land and sea. Consequently, fossil fuels like oil and coal are poised for extinction within the next few decades. The escalation in price of crude oil in international market is a definite manifestation of this phenomenon. What are the options with humanity after the non- renewable sources are exhausted? The only viable alternative available on a sustained basis is renewable sources of energy, freely available in nature or regress back to the darkness of primeval period. It is estimated that India receives solar energy equivalent to over 5,000 trillion Kilo Watts per hour, which is far more than the total energy consumption of the country. The existing hydropower installed capacity is estimated at 88,500 Mega Watts, at 60 % load factor. Similarly, wind power potential in India is around 45,000 Mega Watts. The power of the Sun, Wind, Biomass, Biogas, Water and Geo-Thermals as potential sources of energy is infinite. The rural sector, particularly villages without energy security is the most potent launching ground for harnessing renewable sources of energy, for bridging the urban-rural disparity.

The time is ripe for a revolution – a comprehensive strategy to provide energy services that enables rural development and consequently reduces poverty. Today, renewable energy technologies offer clean, cost effective, reliable options and flexible delivery mechanisms appropriate for almost any use. Renewable energy-efficient infrastructure, like hybrid and micro turbine systems, provide power without the need for costly grid extension. Fuelled by locally available resources and backed by private sector delivery and ownership, these systems can be designed to meet the needs of customers and operated without draining valuable foreign exchange reserves.

Innovative planners can follow the lead set by computer and telephone industries in providing service "without the wire" or WLL, moving beyond centralized power stations, to an array of decentralized systems better able to serve the specific conditions and needs of customers. Most importantly, policy makers can move beyond the idea of energy for energy's sake, and recognize the critical role energy plays in poverty alleviation and development. In consonance with similar principle, Ministry of New & Renewable Energy, Government of India has initiated a number of policy decisions aimed at harnessing renewable energy. The State Government & the nodal agency would do well to initiate a mission for disseminating information and create awareness among the people, regarding the importance of renewable energy and its immense potential to contribute significantly to the process of rural socio-economic emancipation. The significant feature of the new policy must aim to *provide total energy security to every village* within a specific period. The available systems definitely come with a high price tag beyond the reach of common people. The benefits should percolate down to the economically weaker sections at affordable price.

This transition to smarter energy solutions will not come easily. Although the technologies exist, a range of awareness, policy and regulatory device, financing, standards, and local capacity issues will need to be addressed to ensure effective and sustainable market transformation. Eliminating these barriers is beyond the scope and capabilities of any single entity. It requires the collective commitment of Governments, Financial Institutions, Private sector and Non-Governmental organizations.

Renewable energy can play a pivotal role for sustained development of primary sectors in rural areas like agricultural activities, in spite of the inhospitable terrain and grossly inadequate infrastructure. It is imperative to open the market for agricultural products, and modernize operations in order to more effectively compete with farmers from the mainland. Renewable Energy has to be incorporated in State Agriculture Policy. As rural credit system is not functioning effectively, it is important to formulate a sound strategy for financing renewable energy systems. This can be achieved through cost share matching grants for the purchase of devices like Irrigation & Water Pumps, Solar & Wind Electric Projects for lights and to power modern agricultural equipments, cold storages, milk refrigeration projects, vaccine refrigerators etc.

Education & literary mission can be provided a major thrust particularly distance education in the rural habitations where facilities for education are minimal, and worsened during the last two decades due to high dropout rates among School students. The rate of dropouts can be minimized by improving the standard of education by making it more interesting. The use of distance education will be most viable and a network of Distant Learning Schools can be established all over the State in a time bound manner. Solar Photovoltaic Systems can power these schools for expanding access to education through television and non- television based distant learning tools, like interactive radio and IT.

Improvement in health care facilities & sustaining community health services can be provided the much needed momentum through alternate energy. The rural areas of the region as in other similar areas of the country is characterized by chronic disease, environmental degradation, low life expectancy, lack of basic health etc. Renewable Energy has an important role to play in promoting health and reversing these patterns. Further, these Health Centres will be able to function 24 hours a day and radios will connect the villages to the national telecommunications network, facilitating the work of paramedics and other health personnel. There will be enough energy to power Vaccine refrigerators and PX radios besides purification of water – as untreated water in the rural areas is the major cause of diseases majority of which are water borne, assuming epidemic form on most occasions.

Empowerment of rural women is another major area which can benefit immensely. The energy sector is slowly realizing the importance of gender in policies and programs that result in long lasting, productive benefits for women. In order to achieve success in any schemes/ventures, inclusive approaches to community participation should become the standard practice, ensuring that woman's needs and capabilities are included in development processes. This is mandatory for developing village power strategies, which are gender sensitive and therefore maximize responsiveness to all stakeholders in promoting equitable, sustainable energy solutions. The emphasis on this aspect has to be on improved cooking stoves to reduce consumption of wood fuel, water boiling and treatment facilities, indoor lighting, enhancing other income generating non-farm activities like weaving, handloom & handicrafts etc usually undertaken in the evening and night on completion of farm and agricultural activities. Further, milling and drying projects for dehydration of meat, spices, millet, sweet potato, cassava etc through renewable energy is the need of the hour to improve the socio-economic conditions in the rural areas of Meghalaya. All accessible funds must be utilized judiciously formulating a State renewable energy policy based on need based strategy rather than utilization or misuse of available fund without any benefit accruing to the target group & equipments purchased and dumped at different stores for years.

21

NGT ban on coal mining – a substantive issue of environment, safety and health.

(Issue highlighted in the year 2014)

Northeast India has a good deposit of sub-bituminous tertiary coal. Coal from this region has innate features such as high sulphur and low ash content together with environmental sensitive organic and mineral bound elements. Such characteristics are known to have adverse environmental impacts in course of mining and subsequent consumption in coal based industries. Meghalaya and Assam account for around 75 percent of the total coal reserves followed by Nagaland and Arunachal Pradesh with 20 percent and 5 percent reserves, respectively.

Environmental challenges include large scale landscape damage, soil erosion, loss of vegetation, ecosystem and wildlife habitat, air, water, degradation of soil and agricultural lands, land subsidence et al. Unscientific mining of minerals is posing a serious threat to the environment. In addition to air pollution, problems of AMD (Acid Mine Drainage) are intensely localized in the coalfields of northeast India, where ecology of the surrounding area is badly disrupted.

Extraction of coal was introduced by the British in the Khasi Hills between 1869 and 1874. The use was minimal, restricted to heating of their houses and for cooking. The indigenous population slowly followed the system as actual mining was carried out by them as a normal chore like collection of firewood from the forest floor. However, with passage of time, value of Meghalaya coal began to gain recognition and consequent commercial worth leading to trading of the fossil fuel even before independence. After Meghalaya gained full statehood, large scale mining due to growing demand and trading including export of coal to neighbouring Bangladesh and other states of India gained momentum.

A unique aspect related to coal mining activities was that Meghalaya was the only state in India which was not affected by nationalization of coal mines in 1973. This exclusive exemption gave an added boost to coal mining and trading, as the operation was free from the regulatory ambit resulting from nationalization. The probable reason for the exemption was probably the distinctive land holding system, the autonomy granted by the sixth schedule of the Indian constitution and coal mining being a traditional practice of the indigenous population. Coal and timber became the major source of economic activity and also major source of revenue for the government. While wealth and affluence was a natural corollary, environment became the principal victim together with loss of forest cover. The ban of felling of trees by the Supreme Court in 1996 and the recent ban on "rat hole" coal mining by National Green Tribunal has provided the much needed "breather" to the ailing environment and depleting forest cover.

The ban imposed by the National Green Tribunal on "rat hole" mining of coal in Meghalaya, has on expected lines triggered an assortment of diverse opinions, views, conclusions and above all interpretation according to ones comfort and interest. The NGT ruling to-day has set at rest all speculations with the question by the Chairperson of the tribunal during hearing – "Is the constitution and laws of the land including those related to environment and mining applicable here? In essence the NGT bench agreed that the land and minerals may belong to individuals, (in tune with Supreme Court ruling in 2013 on a case related to landowners of Kerala that land owners own minerals not government) but while undertaking mining, environmental and mining laws including regulations and laid down norms/procedures including safety measures will have to be followed besides eliminating health hazards. NGT was of the opinion that mining can be allowed once all such criterion are met and a working mechanism is in place for actual implementation on the ground. Responding to the appeal of livelihood concern and the potential environmental threat posed by the extracted coal in stock in different districts, on exposure to heavy rains during coming monsoon; allowed transportation subject to complete inventorization by a High Level Committee duly constituted for the purpose. This committee shall formulate the terms and conditions of sale with specific advice to the state government not to utilize a single rupee from the royalty for any other purpose other than reclamation, rehabilitation including health improvement measures in mining areas.

The term "rat hole" mining is actually a misnomer. In mining parlance there are only two principal types of mining – open cast mining where coal is available near the surface and underground mining when coal deposits are available at great depths. Mining in Meghalaya falls under the latter category, with mode of operation being the traditional methods of room and pillar, box and side cutting, long wall etc, since coal deposits are available at great depths and productivity far less than open cast method. In this method over burden is negligible since surface excavation is less and restricted to opening of a small pit. Conversely, open cast mining entails removal of large quantities of top soil which is precious nutrients for successful rehabilitation, afforestation etc besides clear felling of total forest cover and associated ground vegetation. It is estimated that in open cast mining, depending on extent of scientific mining adopted, around 20 - 25 hectares of land is damaged for every million tonnes of coal mined. In addition air and noise pollution is much higher in open cast system.

The biggest shortcoming of the underground mining is the issue of land subsidence and breaching of ground water which in untreated form affects local water availability and quality like low pH, increase in total solids, total dissolved solids and heavy metal concentration. AMD is produced by leaching of sulphide minerals in coal with discharge bearing high acidity, hardness, iron, heavy metal, sulphate contents etc. The interim ruling of National Green Tribunal deals primarily with water pollution resulting due to mode of mining followed without treating the mine water before release, mostly as surface flow ultimately contaminating the water bodies including rivers and streams. Such phenomenon is also evident in case of open cast mining areas of Ledo, Tirap and Tikak areas of Assam, Kharsang in Arunachal Pradesh, situated on the extension of same belt, where pH value ranging from 3.61 to 3.28 on waste and stream water reflects high acidity. Therefore, to conclude that only underground mining followed in Meghalaya is responsible for water pollution is not a correct assessment. It is no doubt imperative that the water discharge of the mines has to be treated at all cost to attain normal characteristics before release. This can be undertaken at affordable investment since most coal mining belts in Meghalaya have adjacent huge limestone reserves. Limestone having basic alkaline characteristics can be most affectively used to treat the acid mine discharge through wide variety of low cost innovative process. Mining has to be associated with simultaneous treatment of water which has to be made mandatory besides full proof safety measures for mine workers.

NGT probably, in my opinion, has erred on two accounts while accounting for the basis in imposing the ban on mining of coal. Firstly, mining is not illegal compared to other states where government grants mining lease for a fixed area and the mining extend much beyond the designated area. Here the land where a mine is situated is usually of individual, clan or community ownership and thus not illegal in nature but definitely not in conformity with environment and mining laws of the land. Henceforth, all mining activities has to undertaken after obtaining approval of the Ministry of Coal, Ministry of Mines, DGMS, including environment clearance of State Environment Impact Assessment Authority and the State Pollution Control Board preceded forest clearance under FC Act 1980. The immediate necessity is for the State Government to draw a comprehensive environmentally benign mine management plan including mine safety and a health assurance and safeguard scheme on scientific lines. Secondly, NGT has based its interim order exclusively on a Detailed Project Report submitted by NEEPCO on dangers posed to Kopili Hydro Electric Power Project(KHEP). The data provided in the report particularly those pertaining to water quality test report and the location of collection is ambiguous. Such data conforming to EIA Notifications, 2006 including schedule the amendments therein, all related studies has to be carried out over all seasons regularly spread over a period of 2-3 years. In this case to cite an example, pH of Umkyrpon, Khleriat is shown as 3.67. The source, season, month and year of sample collection is not given. Since pH value of any source is never constant a detailed study, spread over a prolonged period is important. Moreover, this report states that all rivers and streams which drain the mining areas of Jaintia Hills finally empty into the Kopili River on which the KHEP is located. According to the report, a number of plants and machineries of this hydel project has been affected due to the acid mine discharge into Kopili. However, the report is totally silent regarding the coal mining belt across Kopili River located in Assam, where mining continues till date. These mines are an extension of the Jaintia Hills coal seams.

As environment and water pollution has no geographical boundaries or innate characteristic change with change of State boundary, the report itself is not convincing. A visit to the site reveals that water is directly released to Kopili without treatment unlike the draining from the mining areas in the upper ridges of Jaintia Hills, which passes through various streams and rivulets and exposed to high rainfall before being discharged into Kopili. It is also pertinent to note that the principal source of acid discharge as far is KHEP is concerned, emanates from the sulphur generated hot spring(name Garampani – derived from this phenomenon) located within the reservoir of this hydel project. Hence, it will not be justified to attribute all the ills and problems of KHEP to the mining upstream in the catchments of Kopili. The affect definitely is localized in Jaintia Hills but gradually gets neutralized and diluted as it drains downstream, with only a major river Kharkor emptying into Kopili. Fishing in troubled hot water of Kopili?

Finally, in our country, prohibition and ban on minerals and various products like alcohol has been imposed at different times, either by the judiciary or the respective government, based on valid and convincing reasons. However, implementation of such restrictions has not attained optimal results in most cases, leading to situations where the remedy proved to be worse than the disease. In the process while government stands to lose valuable revenue generation, a parallel economy develops, benefiting private players through manipulation and finding innovative means to swerve from the tenets of the ban or prohibition. It remains to be seen how the scenario unravels in the coming years, if the ban on coal mining continues in Meghalaya.

22

World environment day celebration – mere symbolism?

World Environment Day was established by the UN General Assembly in 1972 to mark the opening of the Stockholm Conference on the Human Environment. The day is one of the principal avenue through which the United Nations stimulates worldwide awareness on environment and enhances global political attention and action. The approach is to provide human face to environmental issues by empowering people to become active agents of sustainable and equitable development and develop a synergy among nations to foster awareness & political attention on environment.

The day is celebrated and observed with a slew of activities all over the world, with specific themes every year. One can witness celebration & observance of the day with the pledge and promise for maintaining pollution free pristine environment. What happens the next 364 days is of little or no concern and devoid of practical intervention on a sustained basis, aimed at healing the ailing environment. One is yet to witness actual implementation of the recommendations emerging from hundred of seminars, workshop & deliberations on environment. There is little to celebrate on the status of our environment except to act and not only ring warning bells once or twice a year.

So are all these celebration & observance once a year, sufficient to educe any tangible result to breathe new life into our endangered environment? A definite no, if all such exercise is not backed by practical action on a sustained basis aimed at healing the ailing environment. The day shall be celebrated and observed by government departments & undertakings, educational institutions, social organizations, boards, societies, clubs et al. There will be essay writing, debates, extempore & art competition blended with seminars, loud rhetoric, launching of new schemes, one off cleaning drives among the slew of both theoretical & theatrical interventions. All the pledge and promise for maintaining pollution free pristine environment is usually forgotten earlier than it took to read out. The realization has to be spontaneous and start as a grass root initiative at our individual homes.

While there is a positive impression in children from such awareness campaigns, many of such functions are organized- albeit grudgingly, because of instructions from higher ups or compulsion of show. In fact children can play a very positive and affective role in reversing the process of defiling the environment. Plastic, to cite an example, should be treated as poison and the concept can be spread by the youth to family, friends and neighbours. Children could be encouraged to rein in violators in the locality. Use of plastic must be declared as public nuisance and made punishable under law with both fine and imprisonment. Again, only waste water must be released from a household to public drains and not loaded with garbage, vegetable waste and plastic and in many cases sewage. All these finally end up polluting our streams and water sources. This is the least we can do, as a beginning, to make our and also our immediate neighbours habitat more habitable and environment benign.

23

Echoes of climate variation.

(Issue highlighted in the year 2007)

The threat of climate change or rather variation as some school of thought articulates and global warming, fuelled by relentless commercialization and excessive consumption, has turned into a fighting ground for both policymakers and concerned citizens. The coming decade is set to determine not only a collective response to reducing carbon emissions, but the entire future direction for international development and the global justice movement. Hills in the North East of India, together with rest of the world are on the threshold of a perceptible variation in climatic conditions. In fact people are actually experiencing the alteration which is slowly but surely gaining momentum. Climate of a place is the average weather that is familiar over a period of time. Such dynamic changes over last 100 years are being studied by scientists all over the world who are finding evidence from tree rings, pollen samples, ice cores, and sea sediments. However the alteration in this region, particularly the declining rainfall pattern in areas receiving highest rainfall in the world, has been abrupt and clearly evident for last few years. Human induced activities are primarily responsible for the speed at which this change has occurred. It has acquired the potential to culminate into serious ecological aftermath.

Climate change will affect agricultural yield directly because of alterations in temperature and rainfall. A warmer climate will change rainfall patterns further and increase in the level of evaporation of surface water and rise in the number of cyclones and hurricanes – a phenomenon witnessed at regular intervals. This, in turn, will affect water resources, forests, and other natural ecological systems, power generation, infrastructure, and human health. Change in rainfall pattern experienced by us is one of the most certain and imminent predictions of climate change, closely followed by disruption of safe drinking water sources. Ecosystems which sustain the earth's entire storehouse of species and genetic diversity are very sensitive to changes in climate. It is high time for environment issues to receive some attention and importance it deserves instead of mere symbolism with focus

on regulated mining, restoring the health of our
water bodies and protecting our catchments.
This is the least we can contribute as an honest
beginning to combat climate change – shadow of
which has also fallen on us.

For many children, the greatest barriers to
education are ill health, poor nutrition and
competing demands on their time. Also, most
rural families in the hills do not have access to safe
water or essential household materials, resulting in
children spending their time collecting these rather
than attending school. Further, hazards, such as
earthquakes, monsoons, flooding, desertification
and natural resource degradation can destroy
family livelihoods, prevent children attending
school or lead them to drop out early. Efforts to
manage the impacts of disasters, climate change
and environmental degradation are important to
reduce disruptions to children's education.

The fundamental requirements for good health
include clean air, safe drinking water, and
sufficient nutritious food and secure shelter—
making the environment a key determinant of
health. Climate change also has the potential to
affect all of these requirements.

The environment and climate change are crucial factors in the viability of water supply and sanitation facilities. In the hill states surface water quantity and quality depend on rainfall, land use and environmental processes within catchments, while groundwater quantity and quality depend on sufficient water recharge and protection from pollution. Good waste management and sanitation practices are essential for protecting the environment from pollution and therefore not undermining poor people's livelihoods. With climate change, drought-affected areas are likely to become more widely distributed affecting water availability.

Climate variation also has the potential to undermine food security. Changes to weather patterns can result in an increase in floods or droughts, damage crops and reduce yields. In South Asia climate change impacts could reduce yields by up to 40 per cent by the year 2050 according to studies by the International Food Policy Research Institute. The impact in hilly terrain is likely to be more severe.

Women's knowledge and role in environmental and natural resource management as well as their role in community decision-making processes are an asset in the global effort to reduce risk and vulnerabilities to disasters. Countries incorporate gender dimensions in national disaster risk reduction strategies. In this context, empowering women is not just a way to strengthen community capacities to cope with disasters but also to build community resilience and, through effective partnerships with local and national governments, can innovate and scale up locally led disaster risk reduction initiatives.

Finally concept of green economy has to be adopted on priority. Green Economy is basically aimed at attaining an economic environment that achieves low carbon emissions, resource efficiency and at the same time is socially inclusive. The UNEP-led initiative, launched in late 2008, provides a comprehensive and practical working mechanism, through analysis and policy support for investing in green sectors and in greening environmental unfriendly sectors. The model also speaks of involvement and influence on individuals.

24

Endangered catchments & water bodies!

(Issue highlighted in the year 2005)

The advent of winter chill in Shillong while causing numbness, also keeps people on their toes and edge of their nerves due to fear of impending water crisis. Blood circulation and pressure heightens, yet movement in pipelines transmitting water is gradually reduced to a trickle. This annual feature is well defined and distinct like the weather variations associated with different season. A stream of explanations and assurances flow during this time of the year from technocrats and bureaucratic sources, even as the plumbers, who play a "key" role in the crisis, exhibit their skill of "digging" deep into hapless pockets only to canalize this scarce resource through well greased pipelines. There appears to be no immediate hope of deliverance for most Shillongites, from this sordid saga.

The water related problems in Shillong has arisen mainly from unplanned use and misuse of natural resources, coupled with their gross neglect and pollution. The problem of water crisis gaining momentum, in spite of high rainfall, can primarily be attributed to rapid decline in the fragile resource base due to various anthropogenic activities. The gradual shrinking of this invaluable natural resource is impinging directly on catchments which are natures indigenous "water reservoirs". These "store houses" have been exposed to over exploitation on account of increase in population, associated with deforestation for commercial felling, diverse land use pattern, pastoral and agronomic activities, shifting cultivation, modern unplanned development and unscientific mining and quarrying. All these activities and much more continue unabated. The authorities responsible and duty bound to protect the catchments including a sizeable section of public are presiding over their desecration, ostensibly on a false belief that with high rainfall all sources will remain perennial for infinity. Nothing can be further from the truth. In hill stations like Shillong, bulk of the rain water flows down the hilly terrain into the plains. There is hardy any effort to restrict such haphazard movement of water by initiating measures aimed at maximum seepage and percolation possible to recharge the aquifers and maintain sustained supply to the "natural stores". Consequently, there has been a major depletion of invaluable water sources. It would cost hundreds of crores of rupees to construct water storage equivalent to what even a few hectares of pristine catchment can store.

The Meghalaya Protection of Catchment Areas Act, 1990 was enacted to provide for the protection of catchment areas with a view to preserve water sources and make related provisions. The Act actually came into force from 15th April 1996, after a hiatus of six long years. The Meghalaya Catchment Area Rules came into being from 21st May, 1996 preceded by formation of Advisory Board for all districts, two years earlier during August 1994 in exercise of powers conferred by section 3 of the Act. A Task Force for each district was constituted on 23rd July, 1996. The Department of Environment & Forests is the nodal department to monitor implementation of the Act/Rules. The paper exercise finally completed, execution was mostly impractical since the Act was conceived in haste, without proper study of ground realities and clarity of purpose, leading to repentance in leisure for a "still born" Act, devoid of legal sanctions. Moreover, mere passing of a law or act is not the solution, but only an instrument for commencement of tangible action to deal with a particular issue. Implementation of the law in letter and spirit is more important. The provisions of an Act or Law have to be disseminated and public awareness created, emphasizing on deterrents and penalty for violation of prohibitory clause(s) of the Act. There are few people in the State who are aware of this Act. There is hardly any instance known when this Act was invoked for imposing penalty.

The Task Force constituted for the purpose has recommended, in some districts, corrective measures from time to time to tackle the denigration of catchments, particularly the water supply scheme of Greater Shillong(Umiew), Umkhen and Lawjynriew-Lumiablot. As the areas within the catchment are either belonging to Raid (Clan), Syiem(traditional tribal chief)) or thousands of private land owners, implementation of the corrective measures have been negligible. A small number of schemes could be undertaken in areas under the jurisdiction of Forest Department in addition to few Clan or Raid land like Mylliem Pdah or Raid Laban leased out to the department. The intricate land tenure and holding system besides ownership status prevalent in the state was not accorded due importance while formulating the provisions of the Act. This one factor has become a major deterrent in bringing this Act into play. The Protection of Catchment Areas Act clearly restricts implementation of corrective measures as per section 6 of the Act, pending declaration of an area as catchment area- either critical or non-critical as defined under section 2 (d) and (i) of the Act. Such declaration can only be made after obtaining consent of land owners in writing as per section 5 of the Act. The Act seldom passes through the section 5 hurdles as assent of land owner is a rare phenomenon. Accordingly, there is no scope for invoking the remaining provisions of the Act ranging from section 6 to section 17 which includes prohibition of activities, offences & punishment, bar on civil suit etc. The forest cover in the catchment of Umiew pertaining to Greater Shillong Water Supply Scheme extending from Nongkrem to Mawphlang is virtually wiped out mainly due to agriculture, quarrying and converting wood into charcoal, with little scope for regeneration of the forest- either natural or artificial. This massive degradation has drastically reduced the water retention capacity of the catchment, resulting in decrease of discharge of the numerous springs, streams and rivulets that feed Umiew. This grim scenario bears ominous portends of extinction looming large over the multi crore Greater Shillong Water Supply Scheme. A comprehensive reclamation package encompassing the entire catchment area, irrespective of the status and ownership of the land can only arrest the journey towards total annihilation.

The process associated with degeneration of catchments related to Lawjynriew-Lumiawblot, Umkhen and the seven municipal sources like Umjesai, located in Raid Laban forest has already been set in motion. It is imperative for the Government to review The Meghalaya Protection of Catchment Areas Act 1990, by incorporating adequate legal sanctions, authority and sweeping powers as far as preservation of catchments and implementation of remedial measures are concerned. In order to achieve this goal, section 5 of the Act has to be amended wherein catchment of all water sources, whether big or small extending to a minimum radius conforming to existing vegetative cover, including watershed of all such sources be declared as critical catchments even without the consent of the land owner and legal status of the land, according to the situation. The balance or part area can be declared as non critical catchments. All catchments in the state will thus have a core catchment area or buffer catchment area. The core areas must be maintained in a manner similar to the sacred forests where all activities must be prohibited. Moreover, the competent authorities or board has to be delegated with powers to acquire any portion of existing land, degraded or otherwise falling within the designated core catchment area without the consent of landowners if necessary, to carry out section 2 (c) of the Act or any of the recommendations proposed by the Task Force. Further section 11 of the Act requires amendment by making penalty clauses more stringent and all offences declared as cognizable. The nodal department must be vested with sufficient powers to facilitate implementation of the Act, particularly settlement of appeal against application of the Act.

The law of the land also gives due precedence to general public interest over individual interest. A consensus based on this concept for water sources requires to be evolved or else we may soon have proliferation of "private sources" in all catchment areas catering to individual needs. This emerging trend is visible in Laitkor areas, where number of water sources in private land has been opened to meet the requirements of a few fortunate ones, while majority of the population from Lumiablot to Demthring, Nonthymmai and extending till Rynjah have to virtually squeeze their water taps or stand in long queues for hours to collect the elixir of life- water. The onus lies with the Government to act positively, before the situation reaches a point of no return. The traditional institutions, District Councils and other Organizations will have to put their act together and decide which is more important- an individual interest or welfare of an entire community. This subject which is gradually coming into sharp focus will influence all future social and economic issues, concerning the indigenous society.

25

Mitigation and climate change.

I belong to the particular school of thought who emphasizes on the phenomenon as variation in climate; rather than the more commonly used term – climate change. Natural disasters are among the principal consequence of climate change resulting in cascading affects on agriculture and horticulture, health etc with co-lateral damage to water bodies, infrastructure et al

The frequency and intensity of natural disasters are on the rise all over the world including our state of Meghalaya. The ability of economically trailing states like us to reduce their vulnerability to natural disasters and limit their fiscal exposure is becoming a priority. Disasters often damage both natural resources and infrastructure such as hospitals, schools, transportation systems, ports, energy grids, water bodies including rivers, agricultural land etc. The priority thus is making critical infrastructure resilient.

From a disaster risk reduction perspective, this is an opportunity to promote investments in infrastructure in Meghalaya built to higher standards of hazard resilience, upgrade its cyclone-proof norms for public infrastructure (including schools, health centres and administrative buildings) and introduce them into state legislation.

There is a great need to improve environmental monitoring and surveillance systems in low- and middle-income countries such as India. New research initiatives should focus on collecting high-quality, long-term data on climate-related outcomes with the dual purpose of understanding current situation and predicting future scenarios.

According to an IFAD study, it is estimated that climate change will affect 132 million worldwide by 2050. According to assessment reports published by the Intergovernmental Panel on Climate Change (IPCC), the impact of climate change will be most severe among developing nations, where the highest risk exposure and the lowest adaptation and risk mitigation capacity would be among the poorest populations of these countries. The latest Climate Change Vulnerability Index (CCVI) also revealed that India is considered among the most exposed countries in Asia to 'extreme risk' from climate change. The main climate-change-related risks that India faces can be classified as changes in rainfall patterns, which will reduce agricultural production; rise in sea levels threatening coastal settlements, availability of arable land and aquifers; increase in intensity and frequency of extreme weather events et al. In addition, climate change would most likely have direct and indirect impacts on human health, nutritional insufficiencies or even widespread hunger, due to food insecurity.

Climate change has drawn the attention of various stakeholders including researchers, practitioners, financial institutions, businesses and policy makers and the public, worldwide. Each stakeholder has been keen to develop various climate change mitigation and adaptation solutions, such as energy efficient technologies, reduction in greenhouse gas emissions, climate resilient agriculture, sustainable energy et al. However, there is painfully little knowledge how to apply risk management and transfer strategies to people in general, and to those at the lowest grass root level. Yet, as the entire livelihoods of this group often depend on agriculture and natural resources exploitation, they could be more vulnerable to the effects of global warming and climate change, in addition to their lower ability to absorb financial shocks. Therefore, it is essential and urgent to develop innovative solutions to suit their needs. As weather patterns become increasingly extreme and unpredictable and with little or no access to formal protection against weather related risks, the poor are equipped with insufficient, often unsuitable coping and adaptation mechanisms. Moving away from low-risk, low-yield techniques also entails higher future costs and risk taking. Stories abound about rural poor that tried newer seeds promising bumper crops which they funded in part through loans with high interest rates from local moneylenders, only to then have failure and be pushed deeper into a vicious cycle of poverty. We need to elaborate solutions that would reduce such a situation. Efficient allocation of financial resources and establishment of effective risk transfer solutions is important for a systematic and integrated climate change adaptation framework which strengthens coping capacity of vulnerable communities.

The National Action Plan on Climate Change (NAPCC) of the Government of India, which lays down the strategic road map for addressing climate change impact, clearly articulates the need for strengthening current mechanisms for climate change insurance. The National Policy Dialogue on Climate Change Actions 2010, supported by Swiss Agency of Development Cooperation (SDC1) / Embassy of Switzerland highlighted the need for development organizations to come out with innovative risk transfer mechanisms as part of the integrated approaches towards climate change adaptation. The objective is to establish a work programme on approaches to address 'loss and damage' associated with climate change in vulnerable developing countries, including a climate risk insurance facility together with other options for risk sharing. Many policies have been taken by the Government of India to help vulnerable people through risk reduction and enhancement of adaptive capacities. Whereas in the past the focus was mainly on sustainable livelihoods and poverty alleviation, in recent years the importance of addressing climate change problems more directly has been acknowledged. National Disaster Framework developed by the Government of India covers institutional mechanisms, disaster prevention strategies, early warning systems, disaster mitigation, preparedness and response and human resource development. The newer policies mandate a more holistic disaster risk management strategy with a priority to pre-disaster aspects of mitigation, prevention and preparedness and new institutional mechanisms are being put in place to address the policy.

Micro-insurance can be a powerful means to reduce the vulnerability of the vulnerable grass root population and enable them to better protect and adapt themselves against the impacts and risks due to climate change. There are two viable options available for developing a micro-insurance scheme to address crop and livestock risks: using commercial insurers or using a community-based model with a possible reinsurance partner. Commercial insurers have traditionally served higher income markets but also recognize the potential opportunities among low-income consumers. Experience has shown that behavioural changes amongst rural populations so as to facilitate the adoption of insurance require a certain amount of insurance education as well as awareness / consensus-building activities. As these are community-oriented by nature, there might be merit in exploring this model.

26

Tribulations of mechanical mining.

(Issue highlighted in the year 2013)

A plethora of theories and legalities – mostly sensible but some senile, rusted or figment of imagination or individual interpretation is put forward on sand mining ban. A few by "all knowing" serving and ex "babus" are just preposterous to say the least. The National Green Tribunal (NGT) order on sand mining ban on river beds is restricted within an earlier Supreme Court ruling in case of Uttar Pradesh in 2012 (reiterated in Feb 2013); while rightly emphasising now on extending implementation of the orders all over the country. Earlier, environment impact assessments (EIA) were needed only for mining projects that were located in an area of 5 hectare or more. This "5 hectare catch" was subject to massive misuse in diversion of forest land for non-forestry purpose. Mining proposals were often officially shown as less than the given area though a much larger area was eventually plundered.

The green court reconfirmed environmental clearance mandatory for mining of minor mineral, including sand from river beds even in areas less than 5 hectares. Most mining activities are in violation of different existing environment benign Acts and Rules applicable all over India.

The impact of sand mining although apparently innocuous, is grave. It ranges from forcing the river to change its course, to affecting the groundwater tables and adversely impacting the habitat of micro-organisms. Moreover, sand is important for ground water recharge while on a riverbed it acts as a link between the flowing river and the water table and is part of the aquifer. Sand acts like a "pitcher" and holds a lot of water. The negative impact of mechanical sand mining far outweighs the economic benefits. The devastation caused by floods in Uttarakhand reflects the affect of tampering with the rivers and their resources. When sand and boulders are removed using heavy machines, the erosion capacity of the river increases. The use of invasive explosives and heavy excavator machines witnessed during a recent "river walk" along Umiew is a cause of grave concern, as river beds shall soon become deep craters.

Experts are also worried about the methods used for mining, cautioning against the use of intrusive techniques such as the use of explosives and heavy excavator machines. When sand is mined using excavator machines and through blasting techniques the results can be destructive. In the Himalayan areas especially sand mining should be carried out manually. Excessive in-stream sand mining causes degradation of rivers, therefore, there has to be periodic assessment of how much sand can be sustainably mined, as the quantity can vary from river to river and within a river from stretch to stretch.

When sand and boulders are removed in an unimpeded way using heavy machines, the erosion capacity of the river increases. Sand and boulders prevent the river from changing the course and act as a buffer for the riverbed.

It is not long ago when sand was by and large extracted manually and what got removed was more than replenished every monsoon by the river. Now "removal" has been overpowered by "mining"; and that precisely is the threat. There is danger of livelihood loss that deserves priority. On the other hand conservation of water bodies is the most vital aspect to attain the avowed goal envisaged in the flagship programmes like "Integrated Basin and Livelihood Development Programme" in Meghalaya where a synergy among agriculture, horticulture, forest and plantation crops and particularly aquaculture is imperative and can be sustained only through measures aimed at protection of catchments, fortification of water bodies, strengthening natural sources and conservation techniques to ensure a sound perennial harvesting mechanism in perpetuity. The flag of the flagship venture can "flutter" only then and adequately take care of all those daily wage earners rendered jobless after ban on sand mining and quarrying.

Enforcing the ban to ensure compliance is the biggest challenge in our State considering the land holding scenario and ownership status. Mining of minor minerals is a state subject and the frontline department to ensure compliance is the mining and minerals department together with district civil and police administration. The onus is on the government to evolve a strategy of convergence among different line departments and autonomous district councils. Court orders are usually treated with contempt till a contempt petition is filed.

27

Green finance & sustainability.

Green finance, or investments that contribute towards a sustainable, low-carbon and climate-resilient economy, has been deduced by experts as a way to drive carbon reduction strategies and achieve sustainable development goals. Green finance covers the financing of investments that generate environmental benefits as part of the broader strategy to achieve inclusive, resilient and sustainable development.

In 2016, G20 heads of state for the first time recognized the need to 'scale up green finance' where governments need to be clearer about the policy signals they send to financiers about their plans for climate action and sustainable development.

The transition to a Green Economy requires long-term investment and sustained financing. Public budgets have traditionally been an important source of green infrastructure financing. But given the strains on public finances, large-scale private investment will be needed for the transition towards a green economy. Governments have a key role to play in strengthening domestic policy frameworks to catalyse and mobilise private finance and investment in support of green growth. It is necessary to better align and reform policies across the regulatory spectrum to overcome barriers to green investment, and to provide an enabling environment that can attract both domestic and international investment.

Green Agriculture

There is no doubt that food production, in general, must grow significantly in the next decades. The Food and Agriculture Organization of the United Nations (FAO) estimates that a 70 percent rise in agricultural output is needed by 2050; which is achievable as agricultural production has always been able to grow along with exponential demographic growth thus far.

However, the success story called "the green revolution" has had its price. Turning more and more land to agricultural uses will have severe environmental consequences, including water shortages, concentration of toxic elements, deforestation, loss of biodiversity, erosion, and more. These negative trends will be aggravated by climate change.

In view of these developments, the importance of the agricultural sector to achieving sustainable development is clear. Agriculture is crucial to reducing poverty, achieving food security and improving economic growth as defined in the UN Sustainable Development Goals. The movement to "green" agriculture has led to introduction of better agricultural practices, energy-efficient technology, institutional innovations to improve sustainable food systems, and access to energy in emerging countries. Sustainable agriculture attends to the triple bottom line of sustainability: people, profit, and planet.

Sustainable agriculture also ensures higher supply of sustainable and organic food along the value chain, reaching the end client. Despite the many positive benefits of sustainable agriculture, it remains extremely difficult to engage socially-oriented financial institutions in the move towards sustainable agricultural finance considering challenges laden with risks.

Preparing institutions for agricultural finance:

For organisations to be successful in agricultural finance, they must have the right policies and processes in place, as well as a certain level of flexibility among financial products and services, so they can be easily adapted to the value chains. Financial institutions also need in-depth agricultural knowledge to understand the value chain and the related environmental and social risks, and to be able to address them adequately. With a proper framework, the potential is enormous.

The Sustainable Agricultural Finance Expansion Programme: The program made visible three pillars of greening agriculture as below:

Institutional sustainability: Scaling up of green agricultural finance requires a strong institutional basis of product and agriculture knowledge at management and staff levels. Under this programme, technical assistance focused on strengthening the institutional base shall ensure financial and environmental sustainability in the long term. Institution building efforts includes strategy development, process design, product development and staff training.

Environmental sustainability: Products that are appropriately tailored to the agricultural target group enhance environmental sustainability. In addition to matching agricultural cash flows, a loan product with seasonal loan repayment instead of monthly payment offers farmers more financial opportunities to utilise their land flexibly, rotate crops to protect soil ecosystems and minimise pest infestation, and implement sustainable land use practices. To encourage sustainable agriculture among clients, the participating MFIs developed and communicated good agricultural practices to their clients.

Financial sustainability: The development of new products laid a strong basis for growth and diversification for participating financial institutions while improving their financial sustainability. The improvement of processes and procedures reduced costs and enhanced the organisations' financial performance. Credit risk was decreased by mitigating harmful business practices. The most notable of these relate to the need for regulatory clarity, a comprehensive diagnostic of institutional capabilities, alignment of products and technical assistance with overall business strategy, and careful, context-specific product design which includes a testing phase.

A technical assistance intervention should not be an isolated operation and should be embedded in a wider institutional perspective or strategic plan. Because it is more difficult to build a rural portfolio than an urban one, MFIs with a rural focus need management that firmly believes in that market and is willing to invest in learning.

Agronomists can provide significant insight when introducing agricultural lending and can help avoid costly mistakes related to technical and practical risks inherent to specific crops or value chains.

Product design is a slow but crucial process, which is why timing for development and implementation cannot be taken lightly. A customer-centric design approach with a deep understanding of the value chains can ensure products are appropriate to local context and farming realities.

The use of digital financial services and data can be an integral part of the product design phase. Going a step further, loan disbursements and repayments can be done through the use of mobile phones.

Eco-Tourism and Green Economy

Tourists are increasingly demanding more attention on sustainability—cultural, social, environmental and economic—from destinations and attractions. The quality of tourist experiences is often in direct proportion to the degree of attention to sustainability, particularly cultural authenticity, protection of natural resource, contribution to local community economies and mitigation of carbon emissions. So tourists want to see the results of what Green Bonds finance.

The United Nations and UN World Tourism Organization had declared 2017 the International Year of Sustainable Tourism following the declaration of the universal 2030 Agenda for Sustainable Development and Sustainable Development Goals (SDGs). The International Year aims to support a change in policies, business practices and consumer behaviour towards a more sustainable tourism sector than can contribute to the SDGs.

1. Inclusive and sustainable economic growth

2. Social inclusiveness, employment and poverty reduction

3. Resource efficiency, environmental protection and climate change

4. Cultural values, diversity and heritage

5. Mutual understanding, peace and security.

Further, issue of sustainable bonds for tourism development and establish a sustainable tourism development fund is also imperative for growth of this sector and attain optimal potential.

28

Forest policy and management.

With demands on forests expanding and diversifying, and the forestry agenda becoming increasingly fragmented, institutions responsible for forest management must compete with and complement other sectoral interests to prove their worth to society. Institutional restructuring is necessary to grasp opportunities and ensure that society's demands are effectively and efficiently provided for. In particular, institutional structures need to reflect transitions in forest policies from timber-focused management to focus on protection, conservation and management for a wide range of goods and services. Traditional forestry institutions operating centralized command-and control structures are becoming increasingly outmoded as natural forests are depleted of timber and demands for ecosystem services such as watershed protection, biodiversity conservation and climate change mitigation increase.

The demand for greater social and economic justice and local participation are growing, and

allocation of rights and responsibilities to local
levels is increasingly seen as key to meeting social,
economic and environmental goals in forestry.
In order to be successful and relevant forestry
institutions need to ensure flexibility, strategic
management capabilities, strong "sensory"
capacities and an institutional culture that
responds to change. Dramatic deterioration in the
extent and quality of forest resources in the region
has led to criticism and questioning of the roles,
objectives and institutional cultures of traditional
state forestry agencies.

In many countries, forestry is accorded relatively
low priority by governments regardless of its
economic importance. The forest policy arena
is also being fragmented by an increasing
diversity of specialist agendas, which further
dilute the prospects for forestry agencies to
provide leadership. In such circumstances, the
development of strong advocates and champions
for forestry within the government is hindered,
and the impetus for change is constrained. A
major objective around the world has been the
rationalization of activities and assets to enhance
the efficiency and international competitiveness
of the forestry sector.

Forests have a wide diversity of stakeholders, each with legitimate but often conflicting interests. A national forest policy, therefore, must meet many of society's needs, not just those of the forest sector. A national forest policy can play an immensely important role in society to achieve national development goals, mitigate climate change, provide a sustainable source of renewable materials, and maintain an intact environment. This is the challenge and opportunity for forest policy-makers today. Forest policies and forest legislation are complementary tools. All legislation, including that pertaining to forests, is drafted with certain policies in mind. Forest legislation, therefore, should be based on and guided by a forest policy, not *vice versa.*

A forest law should ensure the proper distribution and enforcement of rights and responsibilities related to forests. Developing a national forest policy is about accommodating different interests in the use and protection of forests – interests that sometimes conflict. Reconciling conflicting views, identifying common interests and working out mutually acceptable solutions requires good negotiation and facilitation skills. Special efforts are often needed to ensure that the voices of certain stakeholders – such as minority groups, the rural poor, women, youth and the general public are heard.

A bottom-up, participatory, multi stakeholder process is a powerful way to develop a national forest policy: it helps to build a sense of joint ownership of the resulting policy and ensure its relevance in times of political change. While such a process is costly, in the long term a lack of one may cost even more. Many countries use the multi-stakeholder platforms of their national forest programmes (NFPs) to help facilitate a participatory process. Decisions on forests and trees often have wide-ranging effects that go well beyond the forest sector. Ideally, therefore, stakeholders from a range of sectors are involved in the forest policy development process. Such broad participation will give the forest policy greater legitimacy in and relevance to the national development agenda.

Re-allocation of rights and responsibilities in relation to forest resources and re-distribution of benefits and risks has been necessary to promote engagement of stakeholders in managing forests. Shifts towards private sector and village/ community, household and/ or individual ownership mean that many more actors are involved in forestry. Forestry agencies, as they withdraw from field-level activities, must prove their worth by facilitating design and implementation of policy and regulations that stimulate, rather than choke, production of forest goods and services under these decentralized regimes. Over past decades, forest and forestry policies have been formulated to encompass the principles of sustainable forest management in most countries. Policy has, however, often emerged from processes that fail to assess or accommodate stakeholder opinions and the situation on the ground. Policy is also commonly poorly understood or supported by a broad range of stakeholders, especially those at the local level. Despite all the credentials of good forest policy, many are inappropriate for the circumstances into which they were born. Implementation has therefore often been lacking and circumstances suggest that institutional reforms beyond policy and legislative amendments are necessary.

Forestry institutions must facilitate increased production of forest goods and services by relinquishing direct control over forest resources. Shifting to facilitative and regulatory roles while increasing flexibility and responsiveness will involve enormous challenges. Global and regional experiences demonstrate that quantum shifts in forestry often occur due to the emergence of tangible economic, political or social shocks. Forecasts and reasoned argument are often insufficient to effect change, especially where governance is weak and other pressing matters are at hand. Environmental degradation is also often an insufficient catalyst unless acute repercussions are experienced. Nonetheless, there are many steps that can be taken to help precipitate change. To a large extent, assessment of field-level forestry issues and what can realistically be achieved is a first step. Capabilities in terms of human and financial resources and available knowledge, and ability to operate with broader socio-economic constraints, have to be more rigorously taken into account if policy objectives are to be achieved.

29

Traditional wisdom & young environment brigade.

Reclamation of the environment which humanity has defiled over last seven decades or more has to find exclusive priority of each inhabitant of planet Earth. A comprehensive vision is only the first step towards attaining a better environment for the future and an effort to arrest the downhill slide. The situation in north east region of India had been better than many other locales of the country. We were blessed with a dream ecological system including rich bio diversity, well balanced and vibrant. To-day we are precariously poised in losing what nature had bestowed on us and the past generations had conserved with diligence. The traditional custom of the indigenous tribal community whose life was intricately linked to nature had laid down self regulatory stipulations aimed at 'consume with care – concern for others to follow". Regulation for focusing on the main things we consume and waste – water, food, energy and all natural resources like forests and animal products. The classification of forest in the hill states of north east, inhabited for centuries by respective, state specific indigenous tribal communities were meant for a definite purpose, aimed at conservation, to serve the community for generations to come. These are few of the multiple initiatives which have been violated at will to serve interests of a few. The older generations may not have dreamt big but had a clear vision and premonition of how things may evolve with time and increasing population. The practical approach was to ensure enough for ones need and not for the present day unbridled greed, which has prompted such wanton destruction and over exploitation of every sphere of the environment.

Today we are at the cross roads for going against the social tenets laid down by our forefathers. Their vision or rather practical wisdom lies shattered among the ruins of unregulated mining, clogged rivers, and deforested land rendered barren, hill sides ravaged and razed to the ground, polluted water bodies et al. This generation has utterly failed the preceding and succeeding generations. All of us are to blame for this devastation which stares us on the face today. And primarily because we were mute spectators to the all round destruction which goes on unabated. We failed to protest against those who sold out our pristine environment through mining of fossil fuels, abetting and conniving in destruction of our untouched forest and rich bio diversity. Natural wealth and resources has been bartered away compromising the basic needs and interest of the common man. Our river systems and water bodies are more of cess pools and dumping ground. History is replete with examples of how rivers are intricately linked to a civilization; the tradition and custom of a community of people. And look what we have converted our symbols of pride into. We have witnessed innumerable agitations and protests on every issue under the sun except for conserving our heritage of nature's bounty, bestowed on the state generously and assiduously guarded by the forefathers. This generation has no answers for the coming generations, whom we have pushed to the brink of disaster.

Most states shall also witness celebration & observance, few days in a year with the pledge and promise for maintaining pollution free pristine environment. What happens during other days of the year shall be of little or no concern and devoid of practical intervention on a sustained basis, aimed at healing the ailing environment? One is yet to witness actual implementation of the recommendations emerging from hundred of seminars, workshop & deliberations on environment. The theme and follow up action should be to start at least one curative initiative from the host of environment degrading issues afflicting us. There is little to celebrate on the status of our environment except to act and not only ring warning bells once or twice a year.

The penance is to involve the young generation at the school level to build a Dream Team to resurrect our ailing environment. Allow them to dream and take pledges to begin the reconstruction of the ruins left behind by us. It is their efforts only which is the last recourse which bears the potential to enforce consumption with care for a rejuvenated ecosystem. Well-being of our environment and economies ultimately depends on the responsible management of the planet's natural resources. And this can only be achieved by an inspired and conscious young generation.

30

Clean environment; better pandemic resilience!

The hill states of north east has been successful till now, to keep at bay the Corona pandemic attack, compared to other states in the plain belt of mainland India. Hill states/UTs like Himachal Pradesh and Ladakh have also not experienced notable numbers of active Covid-19 cases. Although one school of thought subscribes to air borne spread of the virus, World Health Organization is not in conformity with the theory. With COVID-19 being a respiratory illness, it would be intriguing to see how air pollution plays a role in the acceleration of the pandemic – post lockdown. Driven by this logic and current situation, it could be asserted that high level of air pollution is probably a major cause of spread, heightened by human interferences such as deforestation, encroachment on animal habitats and biodiversity loss. The subsequent lockdown of Hubei province - epicentre of the Corona virus; contributed to drastic reduction in high air pollution that has prevented more people from dying prematurely. The air quality in mainland India is among the worst in the world, and high mortality rates due to these unified risks could have been much higher but for the early emergency lockdowns and restrictions activating significant improvement in ambient air and water quality. This resulted in animals coming out and roaming free while humans are locked inside or distant cities graced with the vision of the Himalayas. An important aspect that the lockdown has proven is that nature can recover fast, if pollution agents are withdrawn. The recent spike all over the country, other than the hill states, after easing of lockdown and movement of migrants, is attributed to be the principal cause of the present increase, registering a national average five thousand active cases daily. Cities and big towns are primary sources of environmental pollution, which worsens the pre-existing health conditions of their inhabitants. Studies have suggested a high correlation between increased majorities of COVID-19 infected persons, being urban dwellers, since the virus transmission affecting the respiratory system first is more pronounced in densely populated locations, with the most polluted air quality.

The COVID-19 outbreak is also environment related; believed to have been caused by the transmission of the virus from animals to humans and the ensuing widespread and uncontrolled movement of infected people. In order to address the underlying factors stimulating spread of this pandemic, it is essential to significantly reduce ecosystem destruction, and rigorously implement climate change counter measures to reduce impacts. Above all, lower incidence of COVID-19 cases in the hills is due to relatively small population together with better discipline and adherence to protocols and guidelines, both at individual and community level, has contributed to keep in check the virus spread. All these factors which are intrinsic to Meghalaya can be turned into strength of the state, in the post COVID-19 setting and by extension the USP for resurgence. People are increasingly reconnecting with forgotten notions of self-sufficiency resulting from age old intricate linkage with nature, of the indigenous community inhabiting the hills.

In any significant crisis, like the calamitous Covid-19 pandemic, a reasonable human response is to want things to return to normal and revert quickly to the way they were before. Regardless of its cause or origin, the emergence of COVID-19 has underscored the symbiotic relationship between people and nature and defiling the equilibrium results in catastrophe like the Amphan & COVID-19 crisis. Both offer a critical opportunity for the environment. Response to COVID-19 has demonstrated what can be done differently and accordingly influencing our behaviour in significant ways, all of which will not necessarily reverse after restrictions are lifted. Through this, we have already overcome an important barrier to behaviour change. The "new normal" may see less unnecessary interstate and international travel after experiencing success with remote online meetings, conferences, and even court hearings. Meghalayans like others have slowly but surely shown a willingness to buy locally, supporting farmers and neighbourhood suppliers as people reconnect with forgotten notions of self-sufficiency. Meghalaya and most hill states and areas of NE comprises of traditional self-contained towns linked to villages in a hub and spoke model. This however, needs restructuring and adaptability, consequent to lessons of the pandemic; all of which preferably interwoven to existing pristine inherent environment of the region for a near perfect balance. Therefore, environmentally balanced, socially inclusive and structurally resilient growth is advocated to meet livelihood means.

Therefore, it is important to identify sustainable solutions that prevent pollution levels from rebounding or reaching higher levels after the crisis subsides. Business looks very different to what it did only six months ago. We can take advantage of this shift. As our state government devise their own policy for introduction of economic stimulus packages announced by the centre, it can harness this opportunity to accelerate the transition to a cleaner economy needed to address climate change. Social, economic and environmental systems are inextricably linked, and major disruptions to these systems rarely occur as isolated events. The primary responsibility in the coming days is to find sustainable livelihood options for thousands returning home and lay foundations for positive change. We cannot go back to business as usual and indulge in old habits and governance system that will inflict further harm on the very people, communities and economies that the stimulus packages seek to support. Challenging times will demand tangible and transparent initiatives and investments. Unemployment and hunger can lead to situations worse than the pandemic.

31

Bridging the inequality of "balance".

"Balance" is one word which is most widely used all over the world, in the subject related to development and protection of environment. However, in majority of such developmental paradigm, including mining and allied activities, a holistic approach for attaining the equilibrium between the both is rarely articulated with clarity nor put into practice with sincerity of purpose. In India there are adequate provisions under the FC Act 1980, which provides for compensatory measures while diverting forest land for non forestry purposes. There are stipulated safeguard under the Environment Protection Act, 2006 & the Environment Impact Assessment Notification, 2006, besides host of other acts like the Water & Air act et al to ensure environment security, with the objective of attaining the much brandied balance. However, implementation and subsequent sustenance including compliance is far below the desired level. Thus, the "balance" theory, at ground zero level, generally remains elusive. Consequently, judicial intervention in forest and environmental matters is a reality which prompted the establishment of National Green Tribunal in 2010, to adjudicate in all environment and forests related violations. The environment bench of Supreme Court has been taking a proactive role in passing orders that impact forest governance. While this may not be an ideal situation, it is a reality. The development trends in the country today are at the cost of the environment because of disregard for forest and environmental laws. Citizens have asked the Courts & Tribunals repeatedly to intervene because clearances required under the Forest Conservation Act or the Environment Protection Act, are often simply not taken or compliance of safeguard measures abysmally low.

The mining industry is one of polarising nature. On one hand, it is a strong contributor to a country's industrial and economic development; on the other hand, it is an industry that causes socio-economic and environmental breakdowns. The mining industry is more so evident especially in low-income and emerging markets that are heavily dependent on mineral-based industries and imports to maintain a healthy economic growth. While the economic benefits of the industry are apparent, mining activities are often followed by environmental degradation, social disruption, relocation and resettlement, and severe impacts on livelihoods of the communities affected. Although the negative impacts of the mining industry cannot be completely ruled out, there is a need to ensure that considerations are being made towards the environmental, social and economic dimensions, which are the three pillars of sustainability. The onus to ensure this balance between the economic benefit and sustainable development lies in the hands of the mining firms, through consultations with the policy makers and the communities involved. This is where Corporate Social Responsibility can play a key role.

With India setting a mandatory minimum spending on CSR activities to enable a more effective flow of capital towards tackling the country's developmental challenges, it has put the private sector at the forefront of affecting a more intentional approach towards their CSR activities. In the mining industry, this could mean moving away from short-term, superficial and reactive CSR measures to a more integrated CSR strategy that fulfils not only the regulatory requirements, but also creates holistic and positive environmental and social outcomes.

To steer away from short-term CSR initiatives that provide a Band-Aid effect, it is important for mining firms to conduct Environmental Impact Assessment and Social Impact Assessment to understand the full extent of the effects that the mining activities will have on the environment and the communities. This understanding will then inform future courses of action that should run parallel to stakeholder consultations and open communications with all parties involved, including the government, communities and civil society. The CSR strategies should clearly demonstrate accountability towards the communities in which the mining firms operate in and move towards interventions that fosters sustainable livelihoods and environmental restoration and rehabilitation.

Zooming in on one north-eastern state in India, Meghalaya, a state that is rich in minerals such as coal, limestone, clay, granite, iron ore et al. This mineral-rich repository opens up opportunities for corporate and mining firms to carry out mining activities in the state. This has created avenues for private sector players in the mining industry to set up bases in the state with active CSR activities in the areas affected by mining activities. These interventions include, but not limited to development activities in the affected communities, which include education, agriculture, health and economic empowerment.

However, most of the CSR activities are not directly linked to restore the adverse affect, on the environment, resulting from activities like mining. The interventions are not designed to repair the loss but more focussed on providing immediate general needs, which may be a priority and populist in nature, but in no way connected to compensate the loss of natural resources and associated impairment to the environment and forest status. Therefore, more needs to be done in implementing interventions that will address the loss of natural resources and environmental degradation. Under section 135 of the Companies Act, 2013 deals with CSR, and Schedule VII of the Act lists out the activities which may be included by companies in the CSR policies. The concept of CSR in India as provided in the Companies Act, 2013 and covered under the companies of

CSR policy Rules, 2014, the companies having operating projects and making a net profit are subjected to invest a meagre 2% of the net profit. Hence CSR is exclusively linked to profit.

In such a scenario, which is heavily tilted against the environment in the "balance" hypothesis, introduction of Corporate Environment Responsibility(CSR) is a step in the right direction, subject to proper and systemic execution. The word corporate is also applicable to individual entrepreneurs. CER is not linked to profit but on the capital investment, with flexibility in percentage of allocation, which is determined by the authorized expert bodies, depending on the extent of impingement on the environment arising out of a particular project. The percentage of CER is subject to proper diligence, quantification, and justification. The appraisal authority for each individual project makes a clear suggestion for the specific activities to be carried out under CER on actual requirement at ground level. Such an approach is definitely more realistic, eco friendly and need based intervention. CER refers to the responsibility of a company to ensure a positive impact primarily on the environment and related entities like consumers, employees, communities, stakeholders, and all problems related to the public sphere. The CER activities are increasingly being taken up by the project proponents not only as fulfilling of mandatory provisions but also for the formation and or enhancement of the brand image. Sustainable development has many important facets which include social, economic, and environmental. These components are closely interrelated and mutually reinforcing. CER allocation is formulated to include the cost envisaged for the implementation of the Environment Impact Assessment (EIA) study and Environment Management Plan(EMP) which includes the measures for pollution control, environmental protection, and conservation, rehabilitation and resettlement, wildlife and forest conservation measures including the net present value (NPV) and compensatory afforestation, and other allied activities. The activities proposed under CER are based on the issues raised during the public hearing, social need assessment, rehabilitation and resettlement plan, and EMP. The proposed activity has given restrictions to the affected area around the project. CER activities provide infrastructure creation for drinking water supply, sanitation, health, skill development, electrification including solar power, solid waste management facilities, scientific support, and awareness to local farmers to increase the yield of crop and fodder, rainwater harvesting, soil moisture conservation works, avenue plantation, and plantation in community areas.

There is provision for monitoring the entire activities proposed under the CER. Third party audit by a neutral agency also needs to be included in the scheme. Increasing urbanization and industrialization put pressure on the natural environment resulting in environmental degradation. Hence, CER contributes to the protection and conservation of the environment and development of the society. Therefore it is important for the State to implement CER in the projects for the protection and conservation of the environment and sustainable development of the people. This approach could be the first step towards narrowing the schism between development and environment.

About the Author

The author, **NABA BHATTACHARJEE**, was born and brought up in the picturesque hill station of Shillong- commonly known as "Scotland of the east", and capital of Meghalaya state situated in north east of India. He joined the Forest service and after two decades of service opted to venture out on his own as an environmentalist and environment safeguard specialist. His passion for conservation of the pristine forest, the once clean and clear water bodies and rich bio diversity of his home state, prompted him to flag and highlight the factors and causes posing threat to the entire ecosystem; both through his writings and practical intervention at ground zero level. He also filed various Public Interest Litigations; most prominent being the case filed in the National Green Tribunal on pollution of the major rivers of the state and steps required to ameliorate their deterioration.

www.ingramcontent.com/pod-product-compliance
Lightning Source LLC
Chambersburg PA
CBHW030433290526
45786CB00001B/270